W9-BZQ-302

YOU DON'T
HAVE TO
IF YOU DON'T
WANT TO

BEN KINCHLOW
WITH JIM DENNEY

YOU DON'T
HAVE TO
IF YOU DON'T
WANT TO

A
JANET
THOMA
BOOK

THOMAS NELSON PUBLISHERS
Nashville • Atlanta • London • Vancouver

*To all those who are living "leftover lives" after spending a
lifetime attempting to please everyone else and you are
now living what's left.*

Published in Nashville, Tennessee, by Thomas
Nelson, Inc., Publishers, and distributed in Canada
by Word Communications, Ltd., Richmond, British
Columbia.

Scripture quotations noted KJV are from The King
James Version of the Holy Bible.

The Bible version used in this publication is THE
NEW KING JAMES VERSION. Copyright © 1979,
1980, 1982, Thomas Nelson, Inc., Publishers.

Kinchlow, Ben, 1936–
    You don't have to if you don't want to / by Ben
Kinchlow.
        p.   cm.
    ISBN 0-7852-7875-3
    1. Freedom (Theology)—Popular works.
    I. Title.
BT810.2.K465 1995
248.4—dc20   95-30990
                                                 CIP

Printed in the United States of America

3   4   5   6 — 00   99   98   97

CONTENTS

You Don't
Have To
If You Don't
Want To

1

I DON'T HAVE TO IF I DON'T WANT TO

It was a long, straight stretch of Florida highway, and the sky was crystal-blue. I could see clear to the horizon, both in front of me and behind me. Every once in a while, a car would appear out of the vanishing point up ahead, gradually approach in the opposite lane, then flash past. I was doing about sixty, and so were the oncoming cars. It occurred to me that if another driver decided to veer into my lane just as we were even with each other, his sixty miles an hour and my sixty miles an hour would add up to a combined impact of a hundred and twenty miles an hour!

Then the strangest thought came into my mind: *Why are you driving on this side of the road, Ben?*

"Well," I replied to myself, "this is the side of the road I'm *supposed* to drive on!"

Then the thought occurred to me, *Do you know you can cross over on the other side of the road?*

"Yes," I said, "I guess I could, but I'm not supposed to."

Then it dawned on me: *Why do all the oncoming cars*

stay on that side of the road? It's almost as if there's a wall built down the middle of the road. But there's no wall—just a little yellow line. That line wouldn't hold back a june bug, much less a great big car doing sixty miles an hour! Yet those guys stay on their side and I stay on my side. Amazing!

I drove a little farther, and started thinking about that yellow line. The asphalt on the other side of that line looked just as smooth and level as on my side. There was no traffic in front of me or behind me. If any cars came along, I'd have plenty of time to get back on my side. Why not just ease on over and drive in the other lane for a while?

Then I told myself, "Now, don't you cross that yellow line!"

But I can!

"You're not supposed to!"

But there's nothing stopping me!

Now, that was a very simple thought, but in its simplicity it was profound. I really could cross that yellow line. I had complete freedom to cross that line and drive in the opposite lane if I chose to.

So I checked the rearview mirror and I looked up the road, down the road, sideways, and all around. And then I ever so gently cranked the steering wheel. The car edged to the left and moved across the yellow line. I had done it. I was traveling in the left lane, the lane reserved for oncoming traffic. Suddenly, I felt my heart pounding. My palms started to sweat. *This is wrong*, I thought. *I'm not supposed to be here!*

I turned the wheel and scurried on back to my lane like a scared jackrabbit. And I wondered, *What was I scared of? Why was my heart pounding? Why were my hands sweating? There's no traffic coming. I can drive on any side of the road. It's perfectly safe!*

So I tried it again. This time, I forced myself to drive

about a mile down that deserted road. Then I pulled back into my own lane and stayed there.

As I continued on my way, it dawned on me that people go through life believing themselves to be completely trapped and restricted by "yellow lines." They think that God has drawn these yellow lines, and that they are impassable barriers. The reality is that most of the yellow lines in life exist only in our minds. We have the absolute and total freedom to ignore those lines, to cross those lines, to cruise along the highway of life on the far side of those lines. That is a God-given freedom we all have—and most of us don't even know it.

That was a revelation, what the saints of old used to call an *epiphany*, a sudden and exciting glimpse into one of the deep truths that God has given us in His Word. Out of that moment of revelation came the theme of this book: our awesome, God-given freedom as human beings made in the image of God.

"I Don't Have To If I Don't Want To"

One of the most frightening concepts to ever strike the human mind is that of *individual freedom*, the concept of the absolute liberty we have as human beings. I'm not talking here about our Christian liberty, the enormous freedom that Christians experience in Jesus Christ. We'll talk about that later. What I'm talking about here is the breathtaking, pulse-pounding freedom every human being on this planet has been given by God.

Do any of us really grasp the profound significance of what God did in creating us? Do we even begin to comprehend the vast horizon of choices and options God set before us when He made us in His own image? Most of us have spent our lives bound up by nonexistent yellow lines —lines that have been placed there by our upbringing, by our culture, by our own fears and sense of inadequacy.

One of the most fundamental and profound concepts arising from the fact that God made us in His image is this: *We all have a totally free will*. This free will can be expressed in the positive: "I can if I want to." And it also finds its expression in the negative: "I don't have to if I don't want to."

We can say "Yes" to God—but we don't have to if we don't want to. We actually have the authority to say "No" to God.

We can choose life and blessing and eternity with God in heaven—but we don't have to if we don't want to. We actually have the power in our own hands to determine our eternal destiny.

You only get one life, and one eternity. You have to say "Yes, I can" or "No, I don't want to." You have to make choices. Once this life is past, once eternity has begun, it is too late to go back. The immense power of choice that God has placed in our hands is both exhilarating and terrifying.

My goal in this book is to help you take a good look at the choices that are set before you—*not* make those choices for you. So many people slide through their lives only semiconscious of the options life affords, feeling constrained by mental yellow lines that don't even exist! Life is full of wonders—and it's hedged about by dangers. We can better appreciate the wonders and avoid the dangers if we understand the wonderful freedom God has given us, and the wonderful beings God has created us to be. In order to understand who we are and what we were designed to become, we need to understand *Who* designed us and *why*.

Made Like God

We are a complicated design, aren't we? Why do you suppose that is? I believe it is because we are made in the image of a very complex and fascinating Creator! When He created us, He made us in His image and likeness— not in the sense that God has organs, veins, arteries, muscles, and other physical components as we have. He is not like us; we are like Him. Like God, we have a mind, a will, a spirit, an eternal dimension that is able to think, feel, and experience life. And since we are made in the image and likeness of God, we need to understand what He is like. If we miss what God is like, then we'll miss what we are like.

That doesn't mean, of course, that we have all knowledge or all power as He does. It doesn't mean that human beings are God, as some would have us believe. But even with our human limitations, we do have many of the same capacities that God has. Here are just a few of the ways we are like God:

Like God, we are creative.

The Bible says that in the beginning, God created the heaven and the earth. And when He created, He produced endless, infinite variety. Just imagine all the thousands and thousands of species of plant and animal life that exist today. Then consider this: Scientists have determined that all the species that exist today are less than 1 percent of all the species that have ever existed! All the species we see around us—from the giraffe to the gnat to the jellyfish to the crabgrass on your front lawn to the 3,000-year-old mighty sequoias of California—are just a tiny, surviving remnant of all the millions of life-forms God has designed and placed upon this planet! God is infinitely creative, and there are absolutely no limits to His imagination and productivity. God the Creator made whatever He wanted to make, however He wanted to make it.

But that's not all! The next amazing concept that flows from the creativity of God is that *we* are creative, too! We can't call worlds and galaxies into existence with a single word like He can—but we can imagine and we can create. We write books and make movies about events that have never happened before. Science fiction writers create strange, unseen worlds and populate them with beings that have never lived in any reality we are aware of. We write notes on paper, then turn those notes into music that can melt the human heart and bring tears to the eye. We draw up plans on paper, then turn them into buildings and freeways and spaceships that fly to the moon.

God is the Great Creator. We are little creators. We are miniature reflections of God's own boundless imagination and His love for making things.

Obviously, that doesn't mean we always make the wisest use of our creativity. We choose whether to put our God-given, God-reflecting creativity to a good use or an evil use. From the human mind come the great works of literature—but also such things as pornographic movies or books which ridicule Christ. From the human mind come both good and evil, Disneyland and Auschwitz, homes for runaway children and houses of prostitution, nuclear medicine and nuclear bombs, new ways to save lives and new ways to destroy lives. God has blessed us with an enormous capacity to create; it is sin that so often turns God's blessing into a curse.

Like God, we have dominion.

God has dominion over the universe; He is the Ruler and Lord over all. In Genesis 1:26, we find that God confers dominion on human beings: "Then God said, 'Let Us make man in Our image, according to Our likeness; let them have dominion over the fish of the sea, over the birds of the air, and over the cattle, over all the earth and over every creeping thing that creeps on the earth.'" God gave man dominion over a vast portion of His creation.

And the moment God gave man dominion was the moment things started to get scary on Planet Earth! Why? Because it was at that moment, at the very beginning of human history, that God introduced human free will, which contained within it the potential for the end of human history.

God said to Adam, in effect, "You can do anything you want to. I give you just one guideline, and you are free to violate even that if you choose. I'm not putting any restraints or restrictions on your human free will." God's statement to the first man still stands today. The human race has no restraints, no restrictions. Even if we choose to violate God's laws, He won't stop us.

We human beings have misunderstood and misused our dominion. To our limited minds, we think, "Isn't this great! God has put me in charge! I have dominion! I'm the boss here!" And we proceed to charge in, seize control, and wreak havoc in so many different arenas of our lives. We fail to understand that having dominion doesn't just put us in charge. *It also makes us responsible.* We are responsible for our relationships, for the conduct of our government, for our business conduct and church conduct. We are responsible for the ecology, for the fish of the sea, the birds of the air, and the cattle, and every creeping thing that creeps on the earth.

Like God, we are immortal.

Human beings are made like God in that we—like Him—are spiritual beings. A spirit cannot be destroyed; it is immortal. In Genesis 2, God creates a man of the dust of the earth (one translation of the man's name, Adam, literally means "red dirt"). Then God breathes into Adam's nostrils (the word for "breath" in Hebrew is the same as the word for "spirit"), and the man becomes a living spirit, a living being. God sets the man in the Garden of Eden and creates a mate for him, a woman named Eve. And God shows them all the trees of the Garden and invites them to eat of any and all trees but one. "But of the tree of the knowledge of good and evil," He says, "you shall not eat, for in the day that you eat of it you shall surely die" (Gen. 2:17).

Now, when God talks to Adam and Eve, these two immortal beings He has just made, and says to them "You shall surely die," He is not talking about annihilation, the end of existence. Death, in the Scriptures, means *separation*, not extinction. Natural death is separation of the spirit from the body. Spiritual death is separation of the spirit from God. Eternal death is separation of the spirit from God forever. So what God is saying to Adam and Eve is, in effect, "If you eat from this one tree, you will be separated from Me."

The immensity of this concept is staggering beyond our comprehension. We are beings who have a beginning, but no end. We hold within our own hands the awesome power to select our own eternal destiny. We cannot imagine the horror of eternal spiritual death, nor can we imagine the wonder of eternal life. Both of these ends are completely beyond our understanding and imagining.

The Bible tries to convey to our limited minds some glimmering of the true nature of eternity—heaven is described as having streets of gold which shine like transparent glass; gates of pure pearl; foundations of precious stones such as sapphire, emerald, topaz, and amethyst; a river like crystal flowing through it. The city of heaven needs no light because the glory of God shines there day and night (see Rev. 21 and 22). The description goes on and on, and every detail is an image of richness and wonder that is light-years beyond any human experience.

We think, *Streets of gold? Gates of pearl? What do I need with that?* Aside from fewer potholes, what practical use is a 24-karat gold thoroughfare? Obviously, there is some astounding aspect of heaven that God wants to convey to us. Knowing that human beings associate shining gold with wealth, beauty, and durability, He used this image to transcend the limits of our understanding and convey to us that heaven is a place of unparalleled wonder and beauty. So He paints an image of heaven as a place where one of the most rare and prized substances on Earth is a mere paving material to be trod underfoot!

By contrast, the Bible describes eternity without God as an experience of undying fire and endless torment. These pictures of heaven and hell are surely symbols which correspond to an even more profound reality. The literal reality of both heaven and hell far outstrip anything we can begin to imagine.

God made us to be like Him and to reign with Him. He created us to be immortal beings, sharing a constantly challenging, thrill-packed, joy-filled adventure with Him throughout the endless ages of eternity.

Like God, we have free will.

God can do anything He wants to without any outside interference. "Who can say to Him, 'What are You doing?'" says Job 9:12. Nobody has the right to question God's decisions and actions. He has absolute legal power and authority. He can do anything He wants to do, any way He wants to do it, as often as He wants to do it, and nobody can challenge Him. He is totally independent, totally self-directed, totally sovereign. Every choice He makes is based on His absolute right as a sovereign free agent to make that choice.

But here's the truly amazing fact: God made us like Him in this regard. He gave us the same absolute free will that He has. No human being can be made to do anything he or she doesn't want to do. Every human being can do anything he or she does want to do—so long as it is physically possible.

Most of us are used to thinking we are limited and restricted when we really aren't. We say, "I can't . . ." when we should really say, "I choose not to . . ." How many times in your life have you said, "I have to go to work today"? The fact is, you don't have to go to work today or any day. If you decide to stay home, God won't pick you up by the nape of the neck and drag you down to the office. Your boss won't send the truant officer over to your house to take you off to work. The government won't send tanks to bust your door down and take you into custody. If you decide to stay home, no one can make you do otherwise.

Are there consequences attached to that choice? Sure, there are! You may get a tongue-lashing from your boss, you may get disciplined or demoted, and you may even lose your job. Every action, every decision has consequences. You may feel those consequences are unacceptable, and therefore you *choose* to go to work even when you would prefer to stay home. Every choice has its fallout, but we *do* have choices.

You don't have to do anything you don't want to, and nobody can stop you from doing what you do want to. This is a profound and amazing thought—and there's an even more amazing truth that flows from this thought: There is only one force in the universe that can make you do anything—*and He won't!*

God has given us free will, the power to make choices and decide our own destiny. I call it *decisionability*. Throughout the Scriptures, from Genesis to Revelation, we see that God continually, repeatedly sets choices before the human race. In the Garden of Eden, God told Adam what trees he could freely eat from, and what tree he should avoid. "Exercise your decisionability, Adam," was God's message to the first man. And in Joshua 24:15,

God sets the same choice before the nation of Israel: "Choose for yourselves this day whom you will serve." In other words, "Israel, exercise your decisionability." In the New Testament, John the Baptist, Jesus, and the apostles all called people to make a choice, to exercise their decisionability.

The ball is always in our court. We are the sovereigns, and it's up to us to either surrender or declare war on God.

Humanity: God's Fingerprint on Creation

Why did God create the human race? When He set out to create human beings, He had a completely blank slate. He had all His creative powers at His command, and He was free to make us anything He wanted to, in any way He wanted to.

Remember, He is endlessly creative. He invented the brindled gnu. He invented the duck-billed, web-footed platypus and the spiny anteaters—the only two egg-laying mammals in the world. He invented the rhino with its indestructible armored hide. And he invented the jelly-like hydra which can reproduce in three ways: by sexual reproduction, or by budding like a plant, or even by being cut in half—both halves grow back their missing parts and become complete new organisms! The endless, exotic variety of the animal kingdom absolutely *shouts* to us about the wonderful creativity of our God.

Now, consider this: How many thousands of ideas and concepts did God imagine before He drew up the DNA blueprint for humanity? After all, He didn't have to make us the way we are. There were endless possibilities available to Him. Amazingly, what He came up with was *us*!

Frankly, if I had been God, I certainly wouldn't have made Ben Kinchlow. But don't laugh! I wouldn't have made you either! If I were God, I wouldn't have come up with creatures that could choose to hate me and cause me pain. Given the choice to invent any kind of creature my imagination could design, I sure wouldn't have chosen to make such pesky critters as human beings.

But I'm not God. He is. For reasons fully known only to Him, God made a decision to create beings who were in the image and likeness of Himself, in order to point to Him and testify to His existence. "Let Us make man in Our image," said God, "according to Our likeness" (Gen. 1:26). Who and what we are testifies to who and what God is. As the psalmist says, "I will praise You, for I am fearfully and wonderfully made;/Marvelous are Your works,/And that my soul knows very well" (Ps. 139:14).

God wanted to create something that would testify not only to His power, but to His personhood. He wanted to create something that would serve not only as a footprint, to show He was there, but as a *fingerprint*, to demonstrate His uniqueness.

————

Who Do We Blame?

Freedom always entails responsibility. If you are not free, you cannot be held responsible.

According to Genesis 2:16, God warned Adam, even before Eve was on the scene, that there would be consequences if he ate from the tree. Adam probably related God's warning to Eve, but God hadn't warned Eve directly. Though she was the first to eat from the tree, when she ate nothing happened. Why? Because she was deceived by the serpent. She ate in ignorance (see Gen. 3:1–6; 1 Tim. 2:14).

But when Adam acted, he acted with full knowledge. He knew what he was doing. Acting in complete freedom from any restrictions, coercion, or interference, Adam reached out his hand, took the fruit that Eve handed him, put it to his lips, and sank his teeth into it. At that moment, Adam deliberately violated God's clear command. Being a free moral agent, he became responsible for his decision.

Ever since that moment, we have all been responsible for our decisions. Like Eve, we're not responsible for actions we take in ignorance—but we are totally responsible for those deliberate and disobedient choices we make with our eyes wide open. And we *hate* being held responsible! We absolutely *hate* it! We want to do what we want to do, but we don't want to be responsible.

Most of us shrink back from that weight. In fact, I often hear Christians *blame God* for giving us this freedom and responsibility! They see that, after Adam and Eve sinned and were driven out of the garden, God placed a guard—an angel with a flaming sword—to keep them out. So the questions these Christians ask is, "Why didn't God put an angel on guard *before* Adam ate from the tree? God could have prevented sin from coming into the world—so sin must be God's fault!"

When we say, "Why didn't God keep Adam from sinning?" we are really blaming God for all the sin and problems in the world. This is nothing new, of course. Fact is, the blame game is the oldest game in the book! When God came to Adam after he had eaten from the tree, God asked Adam point-blank, "Have you eaten from the tree of which I commanded you that you should not eat?" (Gen. 3:11).

And Adam began passing the buck just as fast as he could. "The woman whom You gave to be with me, she gave me of the tree, and I ate" (Gen. 3:12). Note that Adam first blames the woman—but he cleverly reserves the biggest share of the blame for God Himself: "The woman whom *You* gave to be with me . . ." He seems to be saying, "God, if You had just let me live alone, if You hadn't stuck me with that miserable woman, this never would have happened!"

This is what people are still doing today: *blaming God*. But it wasn't God who caused the problem. Right from the beginning, God put the ball in Adam's court, saying, "See those two trees there? This one leads to eternal life, but that one leads to separation from Me. Now, you are free to exercise your decisionability, but if you eat from that one, you'll have to suffer the consequences of your decision." That is no more, no less than what God says to us today: Do as you will, the choice is yours—but be prepared to accept the consequences of your decision.

"Hey!" we protest. "I don't want to accept the consequences! I just want to do my thing!" We blame Mom, Dad, society, God, anybody.

"But if I take away your right to suffer the consequences," replies God, "then you are no longer a free being. You are a slave, a robot. I love you too much to treat you as a thing. I love you so much that I have given you true freedom—not just indulgence and license, but the liberty to make choices and to take responsibility for those choices. I have to let you accept the consequences of your choices or else you are not truly free."

"Then," we plead, "just take away this terrible burden of freedom! Take away my free will! I don't want it anymore! Just program me like a computer! *Force* me to do Your will!"

"No," says God. "It is Satan who forces, not Me."

"But if You hate sin, why do You allow us to sin?"

"Don't you see?" says God. "You are a reflection of Me, made in My image. The moment I interfere with your freedom, I disqualify myself as your Creator. To be true to My purpose in making you, I must let you be like Me, I must allow you complete freedom. I can't *force* you to obey Me or to love Me, because to do so is contrary to My nature, and to do so would be to make you less than I created you to be. It would cancel out everything I designed into you when I made you in My image and likeness."

Innocent Bystanders

We don't really want to be all God created us to be, do we? We don't want the responsibility. We don't want the hassle. We don't want to have to make those tough choices. We don't want to drive our car down a highway with a yellow line down the middle. We want our car to ride on rails, like a train. But life isn't like that. Life is full of choices and options, side roads and back alleys, risks and perils.

There are yellow lines—guidelines—along the route of our journey through life, but there are no rails and no barricades. Our conscience is a yellow line. Our childhood training is a yellow line. The Word of God is a yellow line. But we can cross all these yellow lines if we choose to. They are influences, not barriers. They cannot stop us. They can only warn us and point us in a certain direction.

Whether you are on a two-lane highway or on the journey of life, you are perfectly free to act as if you own the road. People do it all the time. When people drive that way on the highway, you have all kinds of problems, from minor scrapes and fender benders to head-on collisions and twelve-car pileups. When people act that way in life, they leave behind them the strewn wreckage of broken lives, shattered marriages, emotionally wounded children, devastated friendships, divided churches, and countless other forms of damage. These are the tragic consequences of the abuse of human free will.

"But," you might say, "those consequences impact innocent people!"

You got it! Innocent people die every day on highways across the country because someone crossed the yellow line or went too fast or got drunk. Innocent people suffer all the time when other people use their free will to make bad choices. Innocent people died in the Holocaust. Innocent people died at Pearl Harbor and Hiroshima, at Coventry and Dresden. Innocent people died in the Crusades, at the Inquisition, from the slave trade, in the French Revolution, and the Civil War. Almost three hundred innocent people died when Pan Am Flight 103 exploded over Lockerbie, Scotland, in 1988. Millions of innocent unborn babies die year after year because of a Supreme Court-ordered freedom of "choice."

When God placed the power of unrestricted decision-ability in our hands, He never said it wouldn't impact innocent people. It will. And God will hold us responsible for our actions.

God has set before each of us an exciting, thrill-packed journey, leading to a destination that absolutely defies our ability to imagine and comprehend. That is the journey we will explore in this book. We will look at the many powerful, practical, life-changing implications of the amazing freedom God has given us, including:

- How a firm grasp of our God-given decisionability can transform our most important relationships, including the marriage relationship;
- How our God-given freedom gives us the right to fail and the power to succeed;
- How a clear understanding of our decisionability can transform our homes, businesses, churches, and even our nation;
- How we can learn to make wiser, more effective decisions in every arena of our lives;
- How accepting responsibility for our decisions places the "keys of the kingdom" in our hands, giving us the power to break the power of temptation, sin, bad habits, and addiction over our lives; and

- How our Christian liberty actually magnifies the human freedom God has given us all.

A *life without limits* awaits you—a journey of satisfaction and joy beyond your wildest dreams. My friend, the best is yet to be. So turn the page and come along. We're setting off together on the adventure of a lifetime!

2

A TALE OF TWO SOVEREIGNS

In February 1862, General Ulysses Simpson Grant faced one of the most well-defended strongholds of the Confederacy—Fort Donelson, Tennessee. The Confederates were dug in, but completely surrounded by Grant's Union forces. It promised to be a bloody battle for both sides. The commander of the Confederate forces inside the fort sent a message to General Grant, suggesting they negotiate the terms of a truce.

"No terms, no truce," Grant replied. "I will accept nothing less than your immediate and unconditional surrender." From that moment on, U. S. Grant was known as "Unconditional Surrender" Grant.

In the Gospels, Jesus reveals to us that God is an "Unconditional Surrender" God!

A Tale of Two Sovereigns

In Luke 14:31–32, Jesus tells of a king who considers going to war. Now, this king has a great deal of power; he has an army of ten thousand men. But as he looks down the road, he sees that the opposing king is coming toward him with an army of *twenty* thousand men. The first king discovers he is outmanned and outgunned two to one!

So this thoughtful king sits down, thinks the situation over, and says to himself, "Now, I'm a king and this other guy's a king. The question is . . . who is the greater king?" Well, it doesn't take a rocket scientist to crunch the numbers and decide he has a serious problem. "Ah-hah!" says he. "I may be a great king, but this guy is even greater! I should figure out some way to make peace with him before hostilities ensue!" So this king sends an ambassador to negotiate, and the other king's conditions are clear: unconditional surrender.

And that's exactly what happens when a man or woman meets God. Each of us is confronted with a choice: Surrender or go to war.

What God says to us in this example, He said to Adam in the Garden. He implies the same thing throughout the Bible in both the Old Testament and New Testament: Because we are made in God's image, we have complete freedom, total free will. He is the greater King; we are the lesser kings. Because He is the original, true Sovereign and we are made in His image, we are also sovereign—but with a small *s*.

Whoa! Now, this is a startling concept: *We are sovereign!* Your first thought is probably, *Hey! I'm not sovereign! Only God is sovereign!* Yes, God is our Sovereign LORD, and, at first, it seems almost blasphemous to apply that same word to ourselves. But wait, when I say, "We are sovereign," I am not saying that we are all-powerful like God, all-knowing like God, all-wise like God, or all-righteous like God—because we are clearly not. We are human beings with all our very human limitations.

The word *sovereign* has a very specific meaning. According to the *On-line Edition of Grolier's Academic Ameri-*

can Encyclopedia, a sovereign is an individual or a nation that is "autonomous, independent, and free from all external control."

Sovereignty, in short, is the power of self-determination, the power to exercise free will. The dictionary definition of *sovereignty* gives us a deeper insight into Jesus' story of the two sovereign kings. "A sovereign state," says *Grolier's,* "is independent and free from all external control; enjoys full legal equality with other states; governs its own territory; selects its own political, economic, and social systems; and has the power to enter into agreements with other nations, to exchange ambassadors, and to decide on war or peace."

That's the range of powers Jesus describes this king as having in Luke 14! The king is independent and free, and he has the power to decide on war or peace. But when he looks down the road and sees an army twice the size of his own, he decides it's time to exercise his sovereign power to exchange ambassadors and make peace! Implicit in this story is the notion that a king has the right to surrender his sovereignty to a greater sovereign.

The Sovereign You

Throughout the New Testament, Jesus is, in effect, telling us, "I am not saying you are not a king. You are. You are a sovereign individual with a sovereign will, because you are made like Me. But I am the original, the ultimate King, the Sovereign, the Lord of Lords, the King of Kings. Now what are you going to do about it? You've come face to face with it. So surrender or fight. Repent! Put up your hands in surrender—or put up your dukes! You can take all the power, strength, might, creativity, and free will you were created with, and use it for Me or against Me." In other words, "Choose for yourselves this day whom you will serve" (Josh. 24:15).

We can say, "Yes, I surrender," or, "No, I rebel. I will do this my way." That choice is completely up to us. But be aware that rebellion puts us in a position of enmity with God. God never says, "You cannot rebel against Me." If we rebel, He says, "You shouldn't, but okay, have it your way. Now, here are the consequences of your actions." If you choose to go to war, you must be willing to pay the price.

It's important to understand that the gospel message Jesus Christ brought to us was not delivered from a master to a bunch of slaves, or from an inventor to a bunch of robots. It is a message from one Sovereign to another sovereign, from a Greater King to a lesser king. The message of the Gospel essentially is, "Here are the terms of your surrender—and those terms are unconditional. Repent for the kingdom of heaven is at hand. Change direction and follow Me" (see Matt. 4:17).

We do not have to repent. We can cling to our sovereign right of free will and declare war on the Greater King —but we have been warned. The Greater Sovereign, King Jesus, says to us, "All authority has been given to Me in heaven and on earth" (Matt. 28:18). He has demonstrated that authority with miracles and signs and wonders—including the ultimate miracle, the Resurrection. The full extent of Jesus' authority will be demonstrated, as Paul says, "when He delivers the kingdom to God the Father, when He puts an end to all rule and all authority and power" (1 Cor. 15:24).

The lordship of Christ is absolutely central to the Gospel, and that is why so many people vehemently resist the Gospel. They understand that Jesus demands nothing less than the complete surrender of their sovereignty—and that is something they are not willing to give up.

A Holy Paradox

During the tumultuous years of the 1960s, singer-song-writer Barry McGuire lived a high-volume, high-intensity life. He began his show business career as one of the founding members of the New Christy Minstrels, and he cowrote and sang one of the Minstrels biggest hits, "Green Green." He was a musical regular on *The Andy Williams Show* for several seasons. When he began recording rock-and-roll songs on his own, his backup singers were a then-little-known quartet called the Mamas and the Papas. He scored a megahit with his Vietnam-era protest anthem, "Eve of Destruction."

But through this time, even while he had all the money, drugs, and other hedonistic pleasures a man could want, Barry was not satisfied. Throughout those years, he was on a spiritual quest, a search for that indefinable something that would bring him peace and give his life meaning. He spent an entire year reading the New Testament and struggling with God. Barry knew what God demanded of him: total surrender of his human sovereignty. But two things stood in his way: (1) Barry didn't want to let go of control of his life, and (2) he was convinced that he had lived too sinful a life to ever be forgiven and set free.

One night, at the end of this long, painful year of struggle, Barry was with a group of friends in a house in the Hollywood Hills, just off Mullholland Drive. While his friends were watching TV, trying out new drugs, and having a great time, Barry was in a corner, suicidally depressed and talking out loud to God. In fact, he was arguing and wrestling with God. Finally, in exasperation with a God who kept hounding him, not even allowing him to enjoy himself at a party, Barry said to God, "Leave me alone!"

At the moment he spoke those words, Barry felt a Presence depart from him, leaving a dark hole inside him like a bottomless abyss. "No, wait, God!" he yelled. "Don't go! I didn't mean it!"

The Presence returned.

And that night, Barry McGuire gave up the struggle, surrendered his sovereignty, and turned control of his life over to Jesus Christ. Since then he has become a minstrel for the Lord, writing and singing songs in concerts and on albums—songs that tell the story of his life and point the way to Jesus Christ.

Barry's story illustrates the paradoxical situation in which we all find ourselves. We have a hunger for God that was designed into us at Creation. We instinctively want God, we long for Him, we need Him. We want to stop fighting with Him. But at the same time, we have a rebellious nature. We don't want God—or anyone else, for that matter—imposing limitations on us. We don't want to have to deal with God's rules and God's moral laws. We want to do our own thing.

We behave toward God in much the same way children behave toward their parents. Children want their parents' protection but reject their parents' limits. They don't understand that their parents' limits are protective limits. So children are continually testing limits—and, I would add, the patience of their parents. Why? Because, while they consciously want to be free, they instinctively and unconsciously want the security of limits.

A child who grows up without boundaries or discipline usually emerges as a very insecure adult. But if a parent sets clear, consistent boundaries and fair, moral rules, then, even though that child may rant and rebel at the time, that child will grow up feeling secure and loved.

Wide-open freedom is a terrifying prospect to most people, including a lot of religious people. We want to know where the boundaries lie. We want someone to set the parameters, to tell us, "This far and no farther."

When the early pioneers first began settling this country, they had no limits, no boundaries, and no laws. Just an endless horizon and endless freedom. So what did they do? They circled the wagons, put up their wooden buildings, and huddled together in little dinky towns out in the middle of the wide-open range! They elected a mayor, hired a sheriff, enacted laws, and immediately began putting curbs and limits on their newfound, hard-won freedoms—and they called it civilization! They wanted everything to be like the world they had just left.

People are terrified of unlimited freedom, and they will invariably choose dictatorship over anarchy, because they want somebody to be in charge.

We all want to know where the stop signs of life are. We feel secure knowing that somebody (or Somebody with a capital S!) is in charge. But satisfying humanity's hunger for fulfillment and security can only come from total surrender to God. All too many people, however, hand their God-given sovereignty over to something *other* than God, to something much *less* than God!

Why this hunger for surrender? Because God designed us to voluntarily surrender our sovereignty to Him but only Him. When we hoard our God-given sovereignty or surrender it to some lesser god, then the one true God will say to us in sorrow, "No! No! But have it your own way." He gives us the freedom and authority to say "No" to Him—yet when we do so, we settle for the limited horizons of our own wants and desires. But when we surrender our sovereignty to Him, He throws the doors wide open, and suddenly we can see the endless horizons that await those who love Him: peace of mind, healed relationships, freedom from bondage to habits and addictions, the joy of serving in His great cause, a richer, more satisfying life on earth, and an endless, thrilling adventure in the life to come.

Human sovereignty is a holy paradox. It defies rational explanation: The more we give of ourselves to God, the more God gives to us in this life and the life to come. That's why Jesus says that everyone who surrenders "houses or brothers or sisters or father or mother or wife or children or lands, for My name's sake, shall receive a hundredfold, and inherit eternal life" (Matt. 19:29).

We Are Valuable to God

I once saw a Superman movie—I forget whether it was *Superman II* or *Superman III* or *Superman MCXXIV*, but it was one of those. The movie opens with three criminal superbeings who escape from the planet Krypton. They come to earth with the idea that they are going to take over. Once on earth, they start tearing up streets and blowing up stuff and generally terrorizing the populace. Superman, in typical fashion, arrives on the scene and proceeds to protect the people in the streets from these evil superbeings.

The superbeings are surprised that Superman bothers to help these puny earth people. In amazement, one of them turns to another and says, "He really cares about these creatures!"

Another evil being replies, "Maybe they're his pets."

These superbeings didn't understand that people aren't like pets to Superman.

And sometimes we make the same mistake in our relationship with God. We forget that people are not pets to God. We consider how great God is, how vast His creation is, how far above our thoughts are His thoughts, and we think, "I'm so small and He's so big. God is remote and far away—certainly not someone I can relate to face-to-face."

What a tragic misconception! We're not like *pets* to God.

Jesus Christ, the Son of God Himself, took our form upon Himself and died on a cross for us. No human being in his right mind would sacrifice his own life or his child's life to save a dog. I love dogs, I've owned dogs all my life, and I have a great, smart, wonderful dog right now by the name of Sir Jackson. But I would never give my life for Sir Jackson! And would I sacrifice one of my three sons for my dog? Never!

Why, then, would God send His Son Jesus Christ to this world to redeem something that has no more significance to Him than a dog has to us? Answer: He wouldn't and He didn't. He sent Jesus to die for men, women, and children who were extremely valuable to Him. For some reason, known fully only to Him, we were so valuable to God that He was unwilling to do without us. There is something about human beings that has eternal significance.

This brings us to an area of tension that troubles many human minds: Are human beings basically good and valuable or basically evil and worthless? Views runs the gamut.

The truth of the matter encompasses *both* ends of the pole. The humanists are right when they say that a human being is a magnificent, awe-inspiring being with tremendous creative potential. After all, God made us in His own image, the image of a magnificent, awe-inspiring, creative Being.

The Christians are right in their negative assessment of humanity when they say that, apart from God, all of our wonderful humanness will ultimately be wasted and lost. "For what will it profit a man," asked Jesus, "if he gains the whole world, and loses his own soul? Or what will a man give in exchange for his soul?" (Mark 8:36, 37). All of that glorious potential and ability, the reflection of God's own image, will burn up and blow away if a person is not in a relationship with God.

But we must put the whole truth of God together, not just one half or the other. God made us wonderful. Sin made us fall short of the glory and perfection of God. And that's the truth. If all we ever preach is the worthlessness of man, we are cutting our own legs out from under us. We are robbing ourselves of the ability to see ourselves as God sees us. But if all we preach is the wonder of natural man, we despise the cross. We are sinners, and we are saved purely by the grace of God—but that's only half the truth. The other half is that we are made in God's image, and we are valuable to Him.

Going in God's Direction

If you have a beautiful sports car and your map-reader causes you to take that car out on the interstate going west in the eastbound lane at 150 miles an hour, I guarantee you are going to have a problem. If you somehow manage to avoid an accident, you will surely attract a lot of attention from the constabulary. You can expect to hear a siren coming up behind you and see a police officer waving and yelling out the window, "Repent! Repent!" Well, maybe not in those exact words, but that's what he means: Stop, pull over, and turn around.

That's what we are like before coming to Christ. Not a worthless heap; we're very valuable, with a lot of God-given horsepower under the hood, a shiny paint job, plenty of chrome, and nice upholstery. God created us, and we are "fearfully and wonderfully made" (Ps. 139:14). But if we take all that steel, chrome, and horsepower out and drive in the wrong direction, we're going to end up in a horrendous crash! So God calls us to stop, turn around, repent, and get in the right lane.

When you turn that car around and start steering in the right direction, you haven't lost or gained any horsepower or amenities. The paint job is the same. The chrome is the same. Even that funny little pair of dice hanging from the rearview mirror is the same. The very same car is now going in the right direction—with a new map-reader, a new guide.

And that's what God is saying about the human race: "I made you, and you have great potential and ability. But you're going in the wrong direction, you're separated from Me. When you're separated from Me, the end of that separation is horror."

That is the Gospel. Throughout the New Testament, we see that this is the core challenge of the Gospel: Let God turn your life around, read His road map for life, and start going *in* His direction, *under* His direction. It is a challenge issued from the Sovereign Creator to the sovereign, self-directed beings He has made in His own magnificent image and likeness. Nowhere does the Bible ever denigrate humanity, because to denigrate the reflections of God's image is to denigrate God Himself. The Bible presents an exalted image of humanity, which only deepens the tragedy inherent in the fact that this beautiful image of God has been marred and distorted by sin.

I used to be a sinner, no doubt about that. If you want to compare sins, just read my autobiography, *Plain Bread!* (Word Books, Waco, Texas). I've racked up a trunkload of sins in my time!

The Scriptures say, "All have sinned" (Rom. 3:23). *All*, no exceptions. Prior to being born again, *we are all sinners by nature*. Perhaps you still are a bona fide, certified sinner! But once you become born again, that's where it stops. At that point, you can say, "I used to be a sinner, but now I'm saved by grace." Yes, even after being born again, we still sometimes miss the mark. But when we sin as Christians, we know it immediately, because sin violates our conscience and our relationship with God. We know it—and in obedience, we deal with it.

A lot of people feel ruined, spoiled, and made worthless

by their sins. But the same passage which tells us that "all have sinned" goes on to say that we all "fall short of the glory of God" (Rom. 3:23). This verse conveys the image of an arrow that continually falls short of its target and fails to hit the bull's-eye. Sinning doesn't mean you're nothing, it means you've missed the mark. What is the mark? The perfect righteousness of God. So what must we do? Admit our inability to hit the target in our own strength, then turn around, face the target, and aim for the bull's-eye of God's perfection, as God gives us strength to steady our aim!

Choose Any Lane You Want

Right out of the Air Force, I put myself through college as a test track driver for the General Tire Company. I was one of the drivers who drew extra pay for high-speed driving, and I racked up a lot of miles on that Texas track at a hundred-some-odd miles an hour. I did "wear tests" and "failure tests," and I have had a few experiences of wrestling a car to a stop after a high-speed blowout. Driving fast for a living (legally!) is interesting work and I enjoyed it.

Some years later, I got a chance to ride the Autobahn— that world-famous no-speed-limit freeway in Germany. I was a passenger in the car, but I was really wishing I could get behind the wheel, open her up, and drive that concrete ribbon myself. You can drive as fast as you want on the Autobahn. Where there are three lanes, the left lane is totally unlimited—and if your car can't easily top 120 miles an hour, you've got no business in that lane! The middle lane is for those doing 85 or 90. The right lane is the slow lane, for people doing 65 or 70 miles per hour.

The life God intended for us is a lot like the Autobahn. You have a lot of freedom to select your own speed and your own lane. God has given you free will, the same measure of free will He gave to Adam when He said, "Of every tree of the garden you may freely eat; but of the tree of the knowledge of good and evil you shall not eat" (Gen. 2:16, 17). We have many options, many varied and interesting choices, many lanes and speeds we can drive, and many trees from which we can eat—and we can do these things whether or not we are going in God's direction.

God has made us self-governing individuals, with the freedom to make our own choices and decide our own destiny. I believe that is one of the reasons that America— despite some flaws and a few major problems—has been such a wondrous and successful experiment. I believe the framers of the Constitution received a divine understanding of this biblical concept of the sovereignty of humanity —our God-given right to be free and self-directed.

In recent decades, however, we have begun chipping away at the idea of individual responsibility, giving away "entitlements," protecting not freedom but the raw, unbridled license of pornographers, criminals, abortion mills, and other social predators. As a result, the quality of American life and the scope of American freedom have declined.

God's Original Plan: Friendship and Fellowship

Why did God do it? Why would He go through all the pain and trouble to create beings who, although made in His image and likeness, are nonetheless capable of rebelling against God? Didn't God understand the risk He took in making human beings with a sovereign free will?

Yes, He knew.

Then why?

I believe God's response to that question would be: "Isn't it obvious? I created you to have fellowship with Me. I created you to be My friends, My coworkers, to share

My throne and My glory, to reign with me for all eternity."

What an astounding thought! God made us so that we could be His friends, working with Him, living in fellowship with Him, and ruling with Him forever!

Take another look at Genesis 3. Right after Adam—not Eve—had eaten from the tree, the eyes of Adam and Eve were opened, and their innocence was destroyed. What was Adam's immediate response? He ran and hid himself among the trees. Now, trees are often used in the Scriptures to symbolize man. In my opinion, there is symbolic importance to the fact that Adam chose to hide himself among trees, which represent the human race. When we sin, it is common for us to try to hide within humanity— our own humanity ("I couldn't help it, it's a disease, I'm not responsible") or the humanity of others ("They made me do it," or, "Everybody does it," or, "Compared to them, I'm not so bad"). To this day, when we sin, we still try to hide ourselves among the "trees."

So God comes looking for Adam—"in the cool of the day," (Gen. 3:8) says the Bible. Hearing God calling, Adam and Eve run from His presence and hide among the trees. But God continues calling, "Where are you?" (Gen. 3:9.)

Finally, Adam responds. "I heard Your voice in the garden," he says from behind a tree, "and I was afraid because I was naked; and I hid myself" (Gen 3:10).

Consider this situation for a moment. Ask yourself some questions: What was God doing in the garden? Why does the Bible make a point of noting that God came looking for Adam and Eve "in the cool of the day"?

Why did God come to the garden? *Because He was looking for His friend!* He wanted to have fellowship with Adam. He wanted to have a conversation with Adam. He came in the cool of the day, that mellow time of the late afternoon just before supper time. God isn't coming to

Adam like a cop or an abusive parent. He's coming into the garden like a dear friend, dropping by for a friendly chat after the day's work is done.

Is God all-knowing? Of course He is! Did God know where Adam was? No question! Why did God ask where Adam was? He already knew! But God did not want to violate Adam's personhood. He didn't want to trample His friendship with Adam. He didn't come in huffin' and puffin' and blowin' down doors. He came in gently, as a dear, trusting friend: "Adam, where are you?" God knew what Adam had done, but He was giving Adam the opportunity to come out and get it straight. See, that's the way good friends treat each other, even when sin strains the relationship.

I don't think this was the first time God had come to meet His friend Adam in the cool of the evening, either. I think there were many times of close and intimate fellowship before sin came into the picture and broke the relationship. I can just hear the dialogue between them:

"Adam," says God, strolling through the garden about an hour before sunset. "Adam, where are you?"

"I'm over here, Lord! By this stream!"

"Ah, there you are. Good to see you! What have you been up to today?"

"Watching the fish run."

"Oh? Great! Well, how did it go?"

"Wonderful, wonderful! Let me tell You what happened! I ran along the top of those hills, just to feel the wind in my hair. Then I did some walking on the south forty. You should see how the corn is springing up! Then I came over and watched the fish. I even caught a great big one with my hands!"

"What did you call it?"

"I called it a *salmon*."

"Hmm. Good name!"

"Then I looked him over and let him go. Lord, those salmon are beautiful creatures!"

"You think so, Adam? Thanks! I thought they turned out rather well Myself!"

"This garden is just loaded with interesting animals, Lord! Seems I discover something new every day. The giraffes—"

"Giraffes?"

"That's what I call those golden animals with the long necks and knobby knees. But I do have one question, Lord."

"What's that, Adam?"

"What's gnu?"

The Lord smiled. (It was, after all, the first time around for that joke.)

"No, seriously, Lord, why in the world did You make the brindled gnu?"

(With apologies to all the theologians among us.)

I really think that's how things started out with God and Adam: two good friends who liked to engage in congenial conversation, enjoying each other's company, fellowshipping with one another. You might wonder what the God of the limitless universe might have in common with a limited little human being like Adam. Why would God—Creator of the Universe, Lord of Space and Time—want to have fellowship and friendship with someone as puny and limited as a human being? This question is based on a failure to appreciate the true nature of human beings, made in the image and likeness of God.

I believe God enjoyed talking things over with Adam, because God created Adam with an intellect and emotions that God could respect and relate to. But then Adam misused his sovereignty, ate the forbidden fruit, and broke the fellowship that existed between himself and God. Suddenly, the whole nature of their relationship was changed:

"Adam! Adam, where are you? Adam! Why don't you answer Me? Adam!"

"I'm—I'm here, Lord!"

"Where? I don't see you!"

"Over here. . . . Behind this tree. . . . I'm—I'm hiding."

"Hiding? But why? Adam, you never hid from Me before!"

"I'm hiding because . . . well, because I'm naked."

"Naked! Who told you you were naked? . . . No, Adam! Surely not! . . . Have you eaten of the tree I told you not to eat of?"

And Adam starts making his excuses. What a horrible tragedy—the first tragedy, which set all other human tragedies and sorrows into motion.

One-on-One with God

When God made human beings, He created something He couldn't get in heaven. Angels are truly awesome creatures of unbelievable power and majesty. One class of angels flies perpetually around the throne of God crying, "Holy, holy, holy is the LORD of hosts; the whole earth is full of His glory!" (Isa. 6:3.)

But as wonderful as angels are, God, for some reason, was apparently not satisfied with only angels as companions. Angels, it would seem, did not make particularly interesting friends for their Creator. So God created somebody who could be a friend to Him—a man, and He called him Adam.

Let me ask you: What makes a really good and lasting marriage? Most people seek passion and romance in a marriage, and there is nothing wrong with that! But when the passion begins to wear off and the two partners begin to take a good hard look at each other, many marriages break apart.

Many marriages fall apart when the partners come to the realization that they don't know how to communicate, or they are not well suited to have fellowship with each other. They discover that while they may have been lovers, they have not been friends. In many cases, it's because they are not intellectually well-matched. If one has a doctorate degree and the other didn't finish eighth grade, the odds are high that these two people will not stay together. Also, there is a danger when one works outside the home and the other has no outside interests. They are unlikely to have much to communicate about, and without communication, there is no fellowship.

Personally, I am convinced that God created a being who could (1) choose of his own sovereign free will to worship and obey God, and (2) commune with God and hold a stimulating conversation with Him. You may think, "Come on! Are you saying this whole free will thing boils down to the fact that God just wanted someone to talk to?" Well, obviously I don't want to oversimplify what is manifestly an extremely complex spiritual reality, but yes, I think God's desire for real fellowship—what the New Testament calls *koinonia*—is at the heart of this whole situation. Think how often the Scriptures deal with the issue of prayer. Remember, prayer is not vain repetition or reading ancient compositions or giving God our "wish list." Prayer is communion—the act of conversing and fellowshipping one-on-one with God! Clearly, this is an issue that is very close to the heart of God.

If you have ever been a mother of small children (or if you have talked to a few mothers, as I have), you may have some inkling of what it was like to be God before He created human beings. What is the most common complaint of stay-at-home moms? "All I do is talk to kids all day! I've got to have some adults to talk to!"

Well, the only beings God had around Him before Adam came on the scene were angels! And I'm convinced that angels, no matter how wonderful they may be, are not capable of experiencing the same degree of fellowship and intimacy with God as humanity is. There is no place in Scripture that gives the slightest hint that angels are made in the image of God, or that they reflect God in any way, or that they experience fellowship with God. They serve Him, glorify Him, worship Him, and some have even tried to overthrow Him, but I do not believe they have the kind of intimate relationship with Him that humanity is designed to have.

Two-way Communication

You may be thinking, "Ben, are you saying that God really gets some kind of joy out of hearing me say, 'Lord, please heal me of this illness,' or, 'Lord, please let me make my house payment this month'?"

No, I'm not saying that—because I think that a lot of what we call "prayer" isn't really prayer at all. I mean, can you picture Adam walking with God in the cool of the evening, saying, "Oh, dear heavenly Father, please gimme this, please gimme that." That's not fellowship with God! That's like writing a letter to Santa!

Think of this: How could Jesus spend entire nights in prayer with the Father? What did He have to talk about for so long? I guarantee it wasn't just a long list of "gimmes." He was having fellowship. He was sharing His own feelings, His joys, His pain, His struggles, His hopes, His fears. He was also listening to the Father, seeking direction, comfort, strength, and fellowship.

I see Jesus coming to God and just having one-on-one fellowship with His Father. I picture times when Jesus sat down with the Father and went over the events of the day, just as husbands and wives should do when they come together in the cool of the evening: "How was your day?

Really? Tell me about it. My day? Where do I begin? Well, let's see. To start with, We fed five thousand today. . . ."

We can begin right now to experience the kind of fellowship God intended us to have with Him right from the moment of Creation. But to have fellowship with God, we must learn to communicate with God. That means we need to *listen* to God as well as *talk* to Him. Communication, after all, is a two-way street. What most of us call prayer isn't a dialogue with God—it's a monologue! We talk, God listens, then we go on about our business—"believing" that God got the message and will deliver the goods. For many of us, we may as well be ringing God up and leaving a message on His answering machine!

In order for fellowship to take place we must listen to what God tells us through His Word and through the still, small voice of His Spirit. It is in our two-way communication with God that we begin to catch a glimmering of the beautiful relationship between God and humanity that began—and was tragically lost—in the Garden of Eden.

Back in 1968, I was a practicing agnostic and an angry, militant radical, a student of the writings of black nationalists such as Elijah Muhammad and Malcolm X. I agreed with Marx that religion was the opiate of the people—and particularly black people. I believed that Christianity (especially) was a trick designed to get poor and oppressed black people to focus on the hereafter so that the rich could enjoy their milk and honey on earth at the expense of the poor.

Having earned a third-degree black belt in karate while in the Air Force, I began using my skills to conduct a martial arts and self-defense class at the college I attended. I was assisted in the class by a man named John Corcoran. Now, John was different from most people I had met, and frankly he wasn't very impressive by the standards I applied in those days. Here I was, a hostile, nasty-mouthed, bitter agnostic, over six feet tall, two hundred pounds, sporting a big afro, and a Fu Manchu mustache. And then there was John, a short white guy with only a brown belt in judo. But there was something about this guy. He and I would often end up after class, sitting for hours while I ranted, raved, and railed at him about how racist American society is and how "hypocritical" Christians and churches are. He always listened very patiently and responded very kindly.

One day, John said, "Can I buy you a hamburger?" and I said, "Sure!" We went over to the student center on the campus and I had on my old Air Force fatigue cap, the square one that fit down on my head to my ears, with my afro sticking out around my head. When the burgers came, John said, "Do you mind if I return thanks?" and I said, "Hey, I ain't no heathen!" And I bowed my head.

Then John started to pray. I expected to hear the same kind of praying I had heard most of my life: "O gracious heavenly Father, we gather together and ask Thy blessing on this food . . ." But that's not what John did. He started just talking to God, exactly as if God was right there in the room. I felt an urge to remove my hat and cigarette and look around and see who John was talking to. But I was afraid to look up, I mean, God might actually have been standing there!

The simple sincerity and reality of that prayer was one of the aspects of John's life that ultimately had a major influence on my decision to give my life to Jesus Christ. When John talked about having something called "a personal relationship with God through Jesus Christ," I had a pretty good idea what he was talking about, having seen his relationship in action. That's the kind of fellowship God intended us to have with Him—a daily friendship, made up of time spent talking to God and listening to God.

God didn't design us only for the sixty, seventy, eighty years or so we are allotted on this planet. He designed us for eternity. We cannot begin to fathom what God has done from beginning to end, for as the Scriptures tell us, " 'Eye has not seen, nor ear heard, nor have entered into the heart of man the things which God has prepared for those who love Him.' But God has revealed them to us through His Spirit" (1 Cor. 2:9, 10). Ecclesiastes also reminds us, "He has put eternity in [our] hearts" (Eccl. 3:11). We are eternal beings with eternal longings. We want to live forever, explore the infinite, and experience the ultimate because God has placed eternity in our hearts, and nothing less than fellowship with the Lord of Eternity will suffice.

In our God-given sovereignty, we can choose to make war on Him, or we can choose friendship with Him. God created us with eternity in mind, and either choice has consequences that last for eternity.

In the next chapter, we will examine one of the most practical, profound, and exciting concepts in Scripture—a concept which flows directly from our human sovereignty and decisionability: the keys of the kingdom.

3

THE KEYS OF THE KINGDOM

It was an early spring morning in 1976, and I had just awakened in my hotel room in Jerusalem, in what is now part of the West Bank, Israel. I got up, showered and dressed, then checked the clock. I still had more than half an hour before it was time to catch the tour bus, so I lay back down on the bed for a few minutes, and was instantly asleep. I immediately began to dream—and to this day, I am convinced that this dream was from God.

In the dream, I saw three men walking in a wooded glen. The scene was so beautiful it suggested to me the Garden of Eden. The woods were shaded, but shafts of golden sunlight cast a warm glow where the three men walked. Somehow, I knew who these three "men" were (though they were not really men at all): the Father, the Son, and the Holy Spirit. I don't know how I knew, but I knew. I'm not sure if I was following them on the road, or if I was looking at this scene from somewhere outside it, but I could see and hear everything that was happening very clearly. Jesus was speaking to the Father, and I could hear Him distinctly.

"I want to give to Harvey Ben," He said, "Matthew 16:19." When he said it in that way, I knew He really meant business. I woke up in a sweat, with my heart pounding and my hands trembling. I jumped up and grabbed my Bible off the dresser—then I paused. Did I really want to know what was in Matthew 16:19? What if it said, "Woe to you, scribes and Pharisees, hypocrites! You whitewashed tombs full of dead men's bones!" Oh, no!

But I had to know, so I opened my Bible and looked up the verse. I should note here that Matthew 16:19 was not a familiar verse to me back then. And it was clear to me that Jesus had specifically said Matthew 16:19—not verse 18 or verse 20 or somewhere in chapter 16. It was verse 19, period. So, with genuine fear and trembling, I opened my Bible to verse 19 and read these words, spoken by Jesus:

> And I will give you the keys of the kingdom of heaven, and whatever you bind on earth will be bound in heaven, and whatever you loose on earth will be loosed in heaven (Matt. 16:19).

What could that mean? Why was Jesus giving me this verse? I didn't understand it—but I began to practice it.

For the next several years, I kept meditating on that verse, again and again. I've since come to the conclusion that this verse is one of the most powerful revelations into who and what human beings are, and what Christians have been granted in the Scriptures. It is a revelation that is intimately intertwined with *who we are* as sovereign beings, made in the image and likeness of God.

Authority and Access

What did Jesus mean when He said, "I will give you the keys of the kingdom of heaven"? I believe the answer will astonish you! In trying to explain to you the enormity of what Jesus did in Matthew 16:19, let me start with a simple analogy.

If you were sitting across from me right now, I could reach into my pocket and hand you a ring of keys. I would say, "These are the keys of Ben Kinchlow." With those keys, you could open my house, start my car or my truck, open my luggage, open my mailbox, get into the dressing rooms, walk right into my private office at CBN, and open my desk. Even if I didn't specifically say where you could go or what you could do with my keys, the simple act of handing those keys over to you would be an act of authorization. I would be trusting you with unrestricted access to virtually every compartment of my life.

That, I believe, is what Jesus did in Matthew 16:19.

Listen closely to what Jesus said: "And I will give you the keys of the kingdom of heaven." Not the keys *to* the kingdom, but the keys *of* the kingdom! Major difference! Jesus is saying—not just to Peter, but to all believers—these are the keys *of* the kingdom in the same way that my keys are the keys *of* Ben Kinchlow. When Jesus handed the keys of the kingdom over to the church, He was entrusting all believers with unrestricted access to every revealed compartment and division and subdivision over which the kingdom has authority. Do you see the magnitude of this concept? He was, in effect, *entrusting heaven's limitless authority to you and me!*

Let that sink in for a moment!

He is saying to us, "I permit you to use this authority as you see fit. Whatever you bind or loose on earth is bound or loosed in heaven." One translation says, "Whatever you forbid on earth, heaven will forbid." The awesome weight of this statement transcends the comprehension of our natural minds.

In the next few pages, we'll see how the implications of Matthew 16:19 apply to such areas of life as:

- Exercising authority over nature;
- Exercising authority over Satan;
- Breaking sinful or self-destructive habits;
- Forgiving others and experiencing emotional and spiritual liberation; and
- Attaining and sustaining motivation for success.

Matthew 16:19—the Lord's revelation of the keys of the kingdom of heaven—is one of the most powerful of all truths that God has revealed in Scripture to men and women. It is a truth that, once fully grasped and apprehended, will *change your life*.

Authority over Nature

A few years after the trip to Israel when the Lord gave me Matthew 16:19, I was again in Israel on one of our CBN tours. During these tours, one of the CBN tour leaders gives a brief talk to the tour group on a boat trip across the Sea of Galilee. I assumed that Pat Robertson was going to give the talk on this trip as usual, so I was just enjoying the ride and the view. A shadow fell on me. I turned, and there was our tour organizer. "Ben," he said, "would you lead us in a brief devotion?"

I said, "Me? Where's Pat?"

"Pat's not on the boat," the man replied.

"What?!" I exclaimed.

"Weren't you told?" the man asked nervously, suddenly realizing that there had been a mix-up. "I mean, I thought you knew Pat wouldn't be on the boat today!"

"Well, no sweat," I said, forcing a big, confident smile on my face. "The Lord will give me something to say." So I made my way up to the front of the boat, silently praying, *Lord, please give me something to say!*

I stood up on a raised area at the bow and looked out at all those faces. The people on the tour were obviously expecting some great words of wisdom. I pointed out to the water and said, "Do you know why Jesus walked across the Sea of Galilee?"

There was a long silence. No one knew what I was going to say next—not even me!

Then I answered my own question: "To get to the other side." The reaction ranged from guffaws to looks of "Did he really say that?"

A twist on a tired old joke? No. You see, that's *exactly* why Jesus was out walking across the Sea of Galilee! Look at the accounts in Matthew 14, Mark 6, and John 6: It was late at night, there was nobody else out there, and He was not there trying to make a sermon illustration or demonstrate a principle. He simply needed to get to the other side! What's the shortest distance between two points? A straight line! He could have walked all the way around the shore of the sea, which would have taken hours, but he decided instead to take a short-cut!

How could He do it? Because He was the Son of God. He had absolute dominion over the forces of nature. As He was out walking across the sea, He came upon the disciples, whom He had sent on ahead in a boat—which was the *usual* way people traveled across the water in those days. When they saw Him, they cried out in fear: "A ghost!" But Jesus didn't want to scare them. He wanted to show them the kind of power they had access to. After demonstrating His dominion over nature, He told them, "Why are you terrified? Where's your faith? You're supposed to be doing this! You have authority in the natural domain!"

Would that I could make this so clear that there would be no way to misunderstand or explain away the incredible reality that this incident represents for you and for me: God really has given *us* this awesome power!

Matthew 17:14–21 and Mark 9:14–29 record the story of a little epileptic boy who is brought to Jesus after His disciples fail to heal him. Jesus is clearly upset—not with the crowd, the boy, or his parents, but with His disciples. "O faithless generation, how long shall I be with you?" He says. "How long shall I bear with you? Bring him to Me" (Mark 9:19).

I recall visiting the island of Bermuda as a young Christian. While there, a man asked me to come home with him and pray for his father, who had been sick in bed for days. I thought, *I'm a minister. I'm supposed to pray for people, right? But hey, I'm on vacation, and you're not supposed to deal with problems on vacation! Besides, I'm not "prayed up" for a challenge like this!* I didn't feel particularly bold or confident about praying for this man's father.

I followed the man to his house, and found his father in a bed, looking very weak and sick. I didn't really expect anything to happen while I was there. However, I went to his side and prayed for him, laying hands on him as I prayed. I was shaken and surprised when, before I had even finished praying, the man sat bolt upright and started to get out of bed. I thought, *Whoa! Easy there, old-timer! You're a sick man! Lie back and get well—but get well gradually like you're supposed to!* Yet this old man felt well, so he just got himself out of bed and was well!

Back in the early seventies, before I joined "The 700 Club," the Christian Broadcasting Network had just moved to Virginia Beach, Virginia. In those days, Virginia Beach was said to be situated in "Hurricane Alley." Killer hurricanes used to whip through that area on a regular basis. CBN had just barely gotten underway, and was operating on a shoestring. The broadcast depended on an old, rickety tower and a lot of other equipment that was exposed to the elements. One day, word came that a massive hurricane was headed straight for Virginia Beach. If that hurricane hit, it would mean the end of CBN, because the broadcast facility would be wiped out and there would be no more money to put up a new one.

So Pat Robertson went to a Full Gospel Businessmen's meeting that morning, and they began to pray and pray. The faith of that group rose, and they actually commanded that hurricane to turn around and go back out to sea. And the hurricane did.

From that time, not another hurricane ever came back through Virginia Beach. There were times when a hurricane threatened, but none ever came through Virginia Beach again—and you never hear people around here talk about "Hurricane Alley" anymore.

We have authority in the here and now, in the natural realm—authority we haven't begun to appropriate, power we haven't begun to realize. And that power only ratchets up as we move from the natural realm—the realm of the forces of nature and human disease—into the realm of spiritual principalities and powers.

Authority over Satan

Back in the seventies, during days of the "Jesus People" movement, I was preaching at a big Jesus festival in a field in Baltimore. I was the last speaker on the roster, so I preached a salvation message and gave an invitation. God's power was evident, and there was a tremendous response of people who wanted to dedicate or rededicate themselves under the Lordship of Jesus Christ. After the festival, I was walking about six inches off the ground (not literally, but that's how I felt!) through the parking lot, heading for my car.

Suddenly I heard someone shout, "There goes Ben

Kinchlow! Ben, Ben! Please, come over here!" I turned and saw an agitated knot of people a little ways away. At the edge of the crowd, a man stood calling to me and frantically motioning to me.

I walked over and said, "What's wrong?"

Then I saw this woman lying on the ground at the center of the crowd. She was having a massive epileptic seizure. The people around her were trying to keep her from swallowing her tongue, her eyes were rolling back, and she was rigid as a board. I didn't even stop to think. I just reached down, pointed my hand at her, and said, "In the name of the Lord Jesus Christ, foul demon come out of her! Woman, be set free!" Instantly, her body went limp, her eyes came down, her tongue came back, and within seconds, she was up and walking around, totally delivered.

On another occasion, following a "700 Club" broadcast, a woman from the audience came to me and said, "Ben, would you pray for me that I would be delivered from cigarettes?" It has been my experience, working with people who are addicted to drugs and alcohol, that addictions are often symbolic or indicative of a deeper problem. I suspected that this woman's addiction to nicotine was a symptom of a much more troubling issue in her life. So I agreed to pray for her, and I brought in a lady from the office (men should never pray alone with women in private, if only for the sake of appearances).

So I prayed for this woman in one of the rooms a short distance from the studio, asking God to deliver her from smoking. The moment I prayed for her deliverance, she screamed, startling me and the lady who had come in to pray with us. The woman flopped on to the floor and began to writhe and froth at the mouth. The other lady and I dropped down on our knees beside this tortured woman and we commanded the demon to come out of her in the name of Jesus. In a few moments, her eyes popped open and she said, "What happened? Am I all right?"

And I said, "Sister, you're better than all right! You've been delivered!"

This incident, and many others I have seen, illustrate to me the fact that God has placed at our disposal an authority, a limitless expanse of power, that we have not even begun to grasp. When this woman was delivered of that demon, I was reminded of the time Jesus sent out the seventy disciples to heal and to preach the Kingdom. When they came back, these disciples were exultant. "Lord," they exclaimed, "even the demons are subject to us in Your name" (Luke 10:17).

And Jesus replied, "I saw Satan fall like lightning from heaven. Behold, I give you the authority to trample on serpents and scorpions, and over all the power of the enemy, and nothing shall by any means hurt you. Nevertheless do not rejoice in this, that the spirits are subject to you, but rather rejoice because your names are written in heaven" (Luke 10:18–20). In other words, "I saw the fall of Satan, and I can see his ultimate defeat. The forces of evil are no big deal. If you want something to get excited about, think of this: Your names are written in heaven! You're going to be among the elite in the big leagues of the universe!"

We have kingdom authority! We are God's designated representatives on earth, carrying out His eternal plan. He entrusts us with this incredible power and authority, and says to us, "If you ask anything in My name, I will do it—uproot trees, even uproot mountains and cast them into the sea! Just remember: You're not what you are because *you* are, but because *I AM*. Your power and your authority exist because of who I AM and what I have designed you to be, as a human being, made in My image."

Breaking Sinful or Self-destructive Habits

I used to smoke more than three packs of cigarettes a day. I tried quitting on several occasions, before and even after I became a Christian. I knew I shouldn't smoke because it was bad for me and it was wastefully expensive. All my Christian friends told me I should quit. So I'd throw my cigarettes out the car window, and within minutes I'd be back slowing down to see if I could find that pack. Yes, it's true that nicotine is one of the most addictive substances on earth, but I can't use the excuse that I was simply a slave to a chemical addiction. In fact, I wasn't convinced God minded my smoking, because I had often smoked while praying, and God never brought it up!

I tried a lot of products, including something I sent away for called Bantron. The idea of Bantron is that you use it as a cigarette substitute, and you supposedly need both Bantron and cigarettes less and less and less until finally you are "cured" of the addiction. But I would take a Bantron—then light up a cigarette right behind the Bantron! Why? Because down deep, *I wanted to smoke.* My desire to quit was half-hearted at best.

Then one day I was reading my Bible and I came across this statement of the Lord Jesus Christ: "If you abide in My word, you are My disciples indeed. And you shall know the truth, and the truth shall make you free" (John 8:31–32). And I thought, *Wait a minute! I'm not free! I can rationalize this all I want to, but I am in bondage to this stupid weed!* Now, I wish I could say I am a person of great willpower, but I can't. I knew I couldn't beat this thing on my own, because I just didn't have the will to do it. Besides, I liked smoking too much!

So I prayed, "God, I refuse to allow this weed to have dominion over me! But, Lord, I have to be honest with You: I just can't do it! I can't break this habit! You have to help me, because if You don't, then I'm just going to continue smoking. Lord, I'm not free, but I want to be free. I no longer give this thing permission to have dominion over me, so Father, I want You to have total dominion over me. Take this stuff away."

At that moment, as I came to the realization that (1) I was in unbreakable bondage to cigarettes, and (2) I no longer allowed cigarettes to keep me in bondage, God was able to line His power up behind my decision. I know this sounds contradictory, but it is really not: Though I knew I was powerless over my nicotine cravings, I made a concentrated decision, a definitive decision—and from the moment I sealed that decision with my prayer to God, I never had another cigarette, never experienced nicotine shakes. Yes, I was tempted to smoke from time to time—but I never yielded to that temptation again. I would quote the Word and remind the devil that I was free.

How was this possible? I believe that when you, as a Christian, make a concentrated decision of your will, you access the keys of the kingdom of heaven. Whatever you bind on earth—including a bad habit or an addiction—is bound in heaven. Once you *forbid* that habit to go on, all of the authority and power of heaven stands behind your decision.

If there is a destructive habit in your life, it will remain as long as you permit it to remain. The moment you determine without reservation to bring to bear your will, your confession, and your authority, that habit has to come to a screeching halt. The moment you say, "No, I refuse to live like this any longer," heaven lines up behind your decision. It's not a matter of willpower. It's a matter of your will and God's power. You supply the will, and God supplies the power.

I knew I didn't have the power to stop smoking, but I made the decision to stop anyway—and I relied upon heaven to back up my decision. In fact, even after I made this concentrated decision, I chose not to throw my cigarettes away. I thought, *I don't want to smoke, but I'm not going to make any rash decisions here! I'm just gonna keep these cigarettes right here in my pocket and carry them around. And Lord, if You lack the ability to keep me from smoking, it doesn't mean I'll love You any less. It just means You don't care about my smoking, so I'll just keep on smoking.*

I kept those cigarettes in my pocket until they got hard, stale, and dry as tinder. Whenever I felt the least little temptation to smoke, I'd say to myself, I don't really want to smoke. As soon as I reiterated my decision, heaven would bolster my will. I never smoked again. I didn't know about Matthew 16:19 back then, and I didn't understand the keys of the kingdom—but that's the "key" that "unlocked" my dependence upon tobacco.

We know that God, the maker of heaven and earth, has the power to *make* us stop smoking. He knows that tobacco is bad for us, that it causes cancer, emphysema, heart disease, nicotine addiction, and all sorts of other problems. He could keep us from smoking in any number of ways: He could send a crop-destroying blight upon all tobacco fields. He could cause all the cigarette-rolling machines in the world to break down. He could have foreseen all the suffering cigarettes would cause and not allow the tobacco weed to exist in the first place. He could even send an angel down every time a person lights up and—*phwooooh!*—blow it right out!

But God will not interfere with our sovereign human will. I've often heard people say, "Well, if God doesn't want me to do this, He'll stop me." But God doesn't do that. If you want to smoke a cigarette, you can smoke that cigarette. God refuses to violate our sovereign decisionability. Instead, He allows us to do whatever we have the moral, physical, and emotional capacity to do—including engaging in self-destructive habits.

Now, what is the habit that holds you down? For you, it may not be smoking. It may be an addiction to alcohol or drugs, a secret sexual habit, a lust for pornography, an eating disorder, a destructive relationship. My friend, you can only remain in your addiction, your sexual shame, your overeating, your anorexia or bulimia, as long as you allow it. You may say, "Ben, you don't know how hard it is for me! You don't know how hard I've tried to be free of this habit!"

Maybe not—but I've seen people become delivered of all of these addictions and habits. I've seen grossly overweight people lose as much as two hundred or three hundred pounds and keep it off. I've seen people kick the addiction to crack cocaine and alcohol. I've seen lives that have done a complete 180-degree turnabout. But I've never seen it happen to people who weren't ready to make a concentrated decision to forbid that habit any further residence in their lives.

Now, I'm not saying you should not get help from a twelve-step group, a support group, a Christian counselor, or a Christian accountability group. These resources can be very helpful in enabling you to seal your decision and hold you accountable. Getting into a group or a counseling relationship can be a sign that you are really serious about breaking that bad habit. The point is simply this: If you are stuck in a shameful, sinful, or self-destructive habit right now, there is one reason and one reason only: *You allow it to continue.* As long as you allow it, heaven will allow it. You will remain mired in that habit until you finally say, "No more! I forbid it!"

Research shows that it takes about twenty-one days to eradicate an old habit or to build a new habit. Practice any action, day by day, for that short length of time, and it will become a habit. So if you want to make a lifelong change in your life, you need to make a concentrated decision and stick to that decision for just three short weeks. Make a commitment and renew that commitment minute by minute, hour by hour—even if you don't believe you have the stamina or the willpower to do so. Practice godly persistence, bind that habit for twenty-one days, and watch as all of heaven stands by your decision, powering your determination, and binding that habit for as long as you bind it.

Forgiveness and Emotional Healing

Getting even—California-style.

Some years ago, a San Francisco–area bank began offering a new service called "personalized scenic checks." While other banks offered the usual check backgrounds —wildflowers, sailboats, and sunsets—this bank allowed customers to bring in a favorite photo of themselves, their children, or the family dog and have it printed on their checks. One man, who had recently gone through an angry, messy divorce, bought a special set of personalized checks to be used only for making alimony payments to his ex. Each check featured a photo of this man giving a big hug and kiss to his new wife!

Here was a man who was creative and imaginative—but also very bitter. "Don't get mad, get even," says the bumper sticker slogan—but the fact is, you can't get even without getting mad. And that kind of "mad" doesn't do anybody any good—least of all you! Resentment tears and twists you up inside. It gives you ulcers and hardens your arteries and clogs your body's immune system with poisons. It robs you of joy and leaves you depressed. As long as you harbor a grudge and a heart full of malice toward another person, you are allowing that person to control your feelings and your behavior.

Jesus gave us an antidote to the poison of resentment. The antidote is something called forgiveness. He knew that "an eye for an eye" would only leave both sides blind; so He said in His Sermon on the Mount, "You have heard

that it was said, 'An eye for an eye and a tooth for a tooth.'
. . . But I say to you, love your enemies, bless those who curse you, do good to those who hate you, and pray for those who spitefully use you and persecute you" (Matt. 5:38, 44).

The problem most people have with forgiveness is that anger is an *emotion* but forgiveness is a *decision of the will*. It is much easier to make a conscious decision than to change an emotion. Mentally, we know God calls us to forgive, that it is in our best interests to forgive, that we can never be healed unless we forgive—but we have a hard time dragging our emotions into line with what our mind knows we should do!

True forgiveness is a *concentrated decision*, an act of your will. You say, "No! I'm not going to allow this! I'm not going to let any other person jerk my emotions around! I choose to get on with my life and leave that pain behind." Every time the memory of that insult or injury comes back to you, you reaffirm your original concentrated decision and refuse to allow hatred and bitterness to take root in your soul. And when you refuse to allow it, heaven will stand behind your decision. Gradually, those feelings and memories will return less and less often, and will be less and less painful, until heaven finally takes all the sting out of your emotions.

"Yeah," you may say, "but you don't know how I've been hurt! You don't know what they did to me!" That's true. But how does what "they" did to you compare with what "they" did to Jesus? And He forgave it all!

If you allow your heart to dwell on bitterness and become all dried out and puckered up, then heaven will allow it too. God will not violate your sovereign will if you make the choice to dwell on your anger. But bind your heart to the principle of forgiveness, and heaven will stand behind you. This is a powerful, revolutionary truth! But then, that's what the gospel of Jesus Christ is: a revolutionary message, designed to transform every aspect of our lives.

The Bible's teaching about forgiveness is not only a *revolution*. It's also a *revelation* of a deep practical and spiritual truth. Preparation always precedes revelation, and God never reveals something to you until, in His flawless judgment, you are ready to handle it and implement it. You are fully capable of implementing the revelation of Christlike forgiveness. You may think you *can't* forgive, that the injustice done to you is too evil, too painful, too outrageous to forgive. But God has a much higher opinion of you than you have of yourself! He knows you are capable of forgiving, and He doesn't allow you to undergo anything you can't handle.

But more than that, you are *responsible* for this revelation you have received. To whom much is entrusted, much is required. When God gives you a revelation, He anticipates that you are going to use this revelation for your own good, the good of the people around you, and the good of the kingdom of God. Forgiveness is the path to healing, and it is the path to pleasing God.

Next, we will see how the principles of the keys of the kingdom apply in the realm of personal goals and career success. God wants us to live abundant lives—and in the next chapter we will discover the power He gives us to live the way He intended!

4

THE FREEDOM TO FAIL, THE POWER TO SUCCEED

When I was growing up, we had chickens. They were called "game" chickens—wild and independent birds who, given the chance, would fly away. So my dad would go out and clip one of their wings so they couldn't fly. The liberty of those birds was completely restricted just by clipping that one wing. We kept those chickens penned up, and my job was to feed them every day. Those birds never had to worry about stormy weather or foxes or any of the other risks a wild bird must face. They had all the food and shelter they wanted.

But they were not free.

God could have treated you and me like those chickens. He could have put us in a nice, safe enclosure, sheltered us from risks and dangers, clipped our wings and restricted our choices, kept us fed and warm and secure. (Some of us would even like that!) But God knows that the moment He restricts us in any way, our sovereign freedom and decisionability is destroyed. God will never do that to us.

As sovereign beings, made in the image and likeness of God, we have the freedom to succeed. But the freedom to succeed always carries with it the freedom to fail. If one is not free to fail, one cannot truly succeed.

Safety Nets and Hammocks

Over two hundred years ago, a historian named Alexander Tyler predicted that our American way of life could not endure, because people do not want to take responsibility for their own choices. In a democratic society, he said, people will invariably hand over their sovereign responsibility and freedom to that government which promises the most benefits. A democracy, Tyler observed,

> cannot exist as a permanent form of government. It can only exist until the voters discover that they can vote themselves largesse from the public treasury. From that moment on, the majority only votes for candidates promising the most benefits from the public treasury, with the result that a democracy always collapses over loose fiscal policy, always followed by a dictatorship.
>
> The average age of the world's greatest civilizations has been two hundred years. These nations have progressed through this sequence: From bondage to spiritual faith; from spiritual faith to great courage; from courage to liberty; from liberty to abundance; from abundance to complacency; from complacency to apathy; from apathy to dependency; from dependency again into bondage ("Michael Reagan's Monthly Monitor," March 1995).

The most chilling statement in Tyler's prophecy is that civilizations rise and fall in two-hundred-year cycles. In other words, *America is already twenty years overdue* for collapse and dictatorship—*and the signs of dependency and imminent bondage are all around us right now!*

The dependency and bondage that Alexander Tyler

predicted over two hundred years ago is encouraged today by politicians, bureaucrats, social workers, and think-tank elitists who pontificate, "We don't want anyone to fail. We are going to make sure everyone has a safety net. It doesn't matter whether you work hard, sacrifice, and struggle—or if you just sit back in your hammock and take it easy. We want everyone to share equally, we want everyone to have everything they want. The government will take care of you. If you don't want to struggle and sacrifice to succeed, that's okay. And just to make sure the successes of other people don't make you feel bad, we'll punish the achievers. We'll take from those who have, and we'll give it to you. The government will take care of you, cradle to grave. That way, nobody fails. What could be more fair?"

That kind of thinking has produced socialism, communism, and the runaway welfare state. The irony is that these "safety nets" don't actually keep anyone from failing. In fact, they guarantee *mass failure* by removing the incentive to work hard, take risks, and succeed. They eliminate the rewards of the Judeo-Christian virtues of hard work, sacrifice, personal responsibility, and thrift. When no one excels, everyone fails. Eventually the people say, "What's the use? I get the same result whether I work or not. I might as well lay back in my hammock and join the non-achievers."

Americans are, by and large, a compassionate people, and we don't like to see people fail. So social engineers eliminate competition and traditional letter grades from our educational system—and then wonder why our students are no longer motivated. They provide welfare and food stamps, call it a "right," an "entitlement," and make these programs better and more inclusive—then wonder why we can't get anyone to take entry-level jobs anymore.

Socialism has been tried, and it has failed. Yet the bureaucrats, pseudo-intellectuals, and social engineers keep trying to make it work in America. They keep expanding the social bureaucracy, and pouring money into a failed welfare system. Thirty years and 5.3 trillion dollars after the launching of the "Great Society" and the "war on poverty," we are farther than ever from the goal of eliminating poverty. You do not encourage people to achieve and become productive by taking away their incentive, their sovereign responsibility, and their freedom to fail.

However well-intended, this elitist, socialist approach to "solving" the problem of poverty actually makes the problem worse. It is a horrible, malignant, degrading thing to take away a person's right to fail. It is an act of enslavement. It is an insult against a person's sovereignty.

God calls us to surrender our sovereignty only to Him —not to another person or to the state. Yes, we pledge our allegiance and our fair share of taxes to our government— but not our sovereignty, not our decisionability. Once we surrender our sovereignty to the government, then government becomes our master—and we deserve just what we get. When we take responsibility for our own lives, our own success or failure, we are the sovereign masters, not the government. And that is how God intends us to live.

Road to Nowhere, Headed for a Blowout

I met the Lord at eighty miles an hour.

Back in 1968, I attended college during the day and drove at the General Tire test track, outside of Uvalde, Texas, from 4:00 to 12:00 at night. We tested tires at different speeds and under various conditions. Some of those tests required speeds of a hundred miles an hour or more. It was interesting work. In fact, there were times—like when a tire would blow at 138 miles an hour—when the job could be downright fascinating!

During that time I was also going through an intense spiritual crisis. God was working on me, (though I didn't know it at the time) and so were a few of God's people. I had heard the Gospel, but I just couldn't comprehend the idea that I could have a "personal relationship" with First Cause, Ultimate Mind, the Giant Clockmaker. To my thinking—the thinking of a dedicated black revolutionary —Jesus Christ was a misguided white Jew who got Himself killed for His beliefs. I could not understand how anyone in his right mind could listen to the teachings of a dead white Jew who couldn't even save His own life.

My whole life was coming apart at the seams. My marriage was crumbling. I went through the motions of my life like a maniac, convinced I had one foot in the grave and the other foot on a grease spot. I figured I was either going to get killed by some irate, jealous husband or I would flip a car on the test track, or I'd fall asleep on the highway. I was in school at 7:00 A.M., teaching a self-defense class at 2:30 P.M., testing tires at 4:00 P.M., then when I got off at midnight I'd often drive forty miles south to Mexico, where I'd drink and carouse till 2:00 or 3:00 the next morning. I'd go back home for an hour or two of sleep, then start it all over again the next morning. It was a cycle of self-destruction, and there were several times I woke up behind the wheel of a car, jouncing onto the shoulder at seventy-five miles an hour.

Looking back, I see that test track as a metaphor of my life at that time: a high-speed road to nowhere, headed for a blowout. I must have been trying to kill myself. For His own reasons, God spared me.

One night, I was driving around the test track, and I started talking out loud to the God I didn't halfway believe in. "God," I said, "I don't really know how to pray. And I don't even know if You're really out there. If You really are there and You can do something with my life, then I'm asking You to come into my life and change it. But don't give me any of this religious business. I've got enough stuff right now to make me really miserable. I don't need any more of that. Give me something *real*."

The Scriptures say, "And you will seek Me and find Me, when you search for Me with all your heart" (Jer. 29:13). And that's what happened to me. It was around eight or nine at night, I was buzzing around that test track with a cigarette hanging out of my mouth, the radio was blasting, and I was talking to God, when *BAM!* Suddenly I *knew* that Jesus Christ is real, that God is there, and that He had changed my life on the spot! All the hatred, self-loathing, fear, bitterness, frustration, anger, lust, and filthiness was washed right out of me—at eighty miles an hour! The mystery of the ages was instantly solved, and I wanted to say something profound to God. But the only thing I could think of to say was, "God, I am so sorry! I didn't know. I just didn't know."

I continued school and working at the test track for a while. I would have been happy working at that test track forever, and preaching weekends, had that been God's plan for me. From the moment I met the Lord Jesus, I didn't have any other ambition than to be a man who loved and followed God. Soon, however, I began to sense God saying to me, "Ben, I have something else for you to do. I have a plan for your life, and I want you to be open to it."

Sometime later, several prominent men came to me and said, "Ben, we've heard about the change in your life, and we want you to consider talking to the young people here on the streets. We want to support you in this, and we'll put some money in an account for you to draw from, so you can minister full-time to those kids." So I went into the General Tire Company office the next day and told the boss I was leaving and why. He thought I was a little off-track, and he said he was sorry to see me go, because he had been planning to send me up to Akron and move me into management. Still, he gave me a letter of recommendation and told me my job would be waiting for me if I ever decided to come back.

I didn't think much about success or failure in those days. I didn't need to. God was taking care of me in a way that could only be called supernatural. The group of men who set me up in ministry never asked me what my needs were. They just contributed to my account as they felt led —but it was clear that God was keeping track of the payables and receivables. If my expenses were only $300 for a given month, then $300 was exactly what would be deposited in my checking account. If I had some extra needs the next month, and my expenses were $1500, then there would be $1500 in the account. There were times when it looked like my income would be exceeded by my outgo— but the Lord always came through. I never had less than I needed, and I never had more. It went on like that for a whole year. God was teaching me His faithfulness.

Then I heard the Lord saying to me, "Okay, Ben, now, I have something else for you to do."

I said, "Okay, Lord. You're the boss. What do You want me to do next? Pastor a church?"

About that time, a fellow came along and offered me a job at a fish hatchery. I said to the Lord, "A fish hatchery?" Well, the work was not as interesting as blowing out tires at a hundred miles an hour, and it wasn't as satisfying as seeing young street people get their lives turned around. But it is absolutely amazing the things you can learn while standing thigh-deep in a scum-covered pond in the Texas heat, skimming green slime off the water and pitching it onto the pond bank with a pitchfork.

For example, I discovered that the reason this scummy green slime had to be removed on a regular basis is that it can kill the fish. If allowed to cover the surface of the water, it robs the water of oxygen and the fish are unable to breathe. And it came to me that sin is like that green slime. It covers your soul, seals off your spirit, and keeps you from "breathing," from experiencing the cleansing, life-giving, restorative exchange of spiritual air with God. That's why we need to regularly shovel the slime and scum of sin off our souls through a process of confession, repentance, and keeping short accounts with God.

Not surprisingly, the same month I quit my street ministry and started work at the fish hatchery, my account at the bank zeroed out. Not another dime came into that account, except what I earned at the fish hatchery. Once again, I wasn't thinking about success or failure. I wasn't ambitious for anything except to do whatever the Lord wanted me to do, and to learn whatever the Lord wanted me to learn.

I worked out there for the summer and learned a lot of valuable lessons. Then, when the summer ended, so did the job. I thought, *Boy, what am I gonna do now?* But the Lord knew what I was going to do next. He led me right into running an alcohol and drug rehabilitation farm. And from there I went right to "The 700 Club." To make a long story short, I have never been unemployed since the day I quit my job at General Tire Company. Every job I took was, as far as I knew, the end of the line, the top rung of my career ladder—yet God has always had something even better and more interesting for me to do just around the corner. Whatever I did, I made my mind up to do it with all my might, as if it would be the job I would do for the rest of my life.

"You were faithful over a few things," said the master to his servant, "I will make you ruler over many things" (Matt. 25:21). I'm certainly not holding myself out as a model of either faithfulness or success; that is for God to judge. But I believe that one thing I have learned over the years is that when we faithfully seek God and His kingdom right where we are, He gives us greater responsibility, greater challenges, and greater rewards. I have to tell you from the bottom of my heart, I could not have designed a more exciting, rewarding, or fun-filled life than what God has allowed me to lead over the nearly twenty-five years that I have known Him. It has been absolutely phenomenal!

So I have come to a conclusion about success that you might find surprising: If you want to be successful, don't focus on success.

First Secret of Success: Seek God—Not Success

God says to each of us, "What do you want from Me?" And some of us say, "I just want a nice car and a big house." And some of us say, "I just want all my bills paid and no worries." And some of us say, "I just want my good health." And some of us say, "I just want to be happy." And some of us say, "I just want to be successful."

There's nothing wrong with having material possessions, money, or any other thing you like. But when God asks, "What do you want from Me?" these answers are all the *wrong* answers! What is the correct answer? "I don't want anything but You, Lord." What is the desire of your heart? "Only You, Lord." What are you seeking in life? "Just You, Lord, Your kingdom and Your righteousness." If there is one truth that has become absolutely clear to me in the almost twenty-five years since I first met God on that test track in Uvalde, Texas, it's this: If you seek Him first, if all your desire is for Him, you don't have to worry about success or money or possessions or happiness. You'll have all you need and more than you can use. The prime example of this principle is that great Old Testament servant of God, Joseph.

Joseph was sold as a slave to Potiphar, an Egyptian master. He could have said, "Aw, man! This is totally unfair! Slavery is unjust! Why should I have to work like a dog for a lousy bowl of gruel and a moth-eaten old cot?

Hey, I'm just gonna do the minimum! I'm just gonna get by!"

But that wasn't Joseph's way. Instead, he said, "I'm going to do everything with excellence. I'm going to serve Potiphar to the best of my ability. I'm going to do all my tasks heartily, as to the Lord." And the result was that Potiphar turned everything over to Joseph. He trusted Joseph with the management of his entire house. If a couple of the other servants got into an argument, or if the gardener wanted a raise, or if a salesman came by selling aluminum siding, Potiphar would just say, "Joseph handles that. Go talk to him."

So Joseph rose to a responsible position—not because he was ambitious for advancement, but because he was ambitious to serve God. Please note: The way he served God was by being totally devoted, committed, and dedicated to the task at hand. He was an Old Testament example of the New Testament principle, "And whatever you do, do it heartily, as to the Lord and not to men" (Col. 3:23).

Of course, Joseph had setbacks to deal with. Potiphar's wife tried and failed to seduce him—then got him thrown in prison. Now comes the pity party and blaming God, right? Wrong! Even in prison, Joseph committed himself to serving God by giving his best efforts to those who were in charge over him. Soon he became a leader in the prison, and the warden turned everything over to Joseph. He said, "Hey, I don't keep track of the little stuff around here. I just turn it over to Joseph."

Eventually, Joseph's character and abilities were recognized. He was plucked out of prison and given authority second only to that of Pharaoh himself. He designed a food stamp program that worked! When people came to Pharaoh wanting a policy decision or a new government program, Pharaoh would say, "Go see my man, Joseph!"

So Joseph—a Jewish kid, a family reject who had come

up from the ghetto of slavery and prison—ultimately made it bigtime in Egypt! He had wealth, he had power, he had a reputation—but it didn't come to him because he sought these things. No, they came because all he ever sought was God and His righteousness. It's the same principle Jesus gave us when He said,

> Therefore do not worry, saying, "What shall we eat?" or "What shall we drink?" or "What shall we wear?" For after all these things the Gentiles seek. For your heavenly Father knows that you need all these things. But seek first the kingdom of God and His righteousness, and all these things shall be added to you (Matt. 6:31–33).

All of these things shall be added to you! All of *what* things? What to eat, what to drink, what to wear! The material necessities and blessings of life!

Now, I can just hear somebody out there saying, "Hold on, Ben! God doesn't want any Christians to be rich and successful! Remember, the Bible says you can't serve God and mammon, you can't serve God and money!" You are partly right—but only partly. Jesus did indeed say, "No servant can serve two masters; for either he will hate the one and love the other, or else he will be loyal to the one and despise the other. You cannot serve God and mammon" (Luke 16:13).

Jesus said you can't *serve* God and mammon. He didn't say you can't *have* God and mammon. Big difference! You can only have one master, and if you love and serve and seek first the kingdom of God, where Jesus is king, then money is your servant. But if you seek first the kingdom of mammon, then money is your king, not the Lord Jesus.

So the first secret of true success is: *Seek God, not success.*

To seek God and His righteousness, we have to make that alone our goal. God will then add blessing and success to our lives. But God will not allow Himself to be used as a means to an end. He deserves and demands our total worship, our total praise, our total servanthood—and He richly rewards those who diligently seek Him.

———

Second Secret of Success: Give Yourself Permission to Succeed

A man and his son were walking down the street when they saw a beautiful white Rolls-Royce stopped at a red light. In the back seat of the car was a man in an expensive suit, puffing on a big cigar. The light changed, the car rolled away, and the man and his son saw a sign on the back of the car that said, "M.D." The father patted his son on the shoulder and said, "See there, son? If you get an education, work hard, and become a doctor, one day you can be successful and ride around in a big car."

The next day, the man and his son were walking and came to the same corner, where they saw a shiny black Rolls-Royce. In the back seat was a man in an expensive suit, sipping a martini. The light changed, the car pulled off, and the man and his son saw a sign on the back of the car that said, "Attorney at Law." The father patted his son on the shoulder and said, "See there, son? If you get an education, pursue your goals, and become a lawyer, one day you can be successful and ride around in a big car."

The following day, the man and his son were again out walking. Coming to the same corner, they saw a gleaming silver Rolls-Royce with burgundy interior. In the back seat was a gentleman in an expensive suit, reading his Bible. The light changed, the car drove past, and the man and his son saw a sign on the back of the car that read, "Clergy."

The father scowled and said, "Look at that crook!"

Sound familiar? Many Christians have the idea that success is a sin, that poverty is next to godliness. They don't feel they have a legal, God-given right to succeed. Yet the right to succeed, the power to succeed, and the permission to succeed are built into our God-given sovereignty and decisionability. As sovereign men and women, we don't need permission to speak, permission to go to the bathroom, permission to leave the room, or permission to succeed. Deuteronomy 8:18 tells us that God gives us the strength, power, and might to create wealth, and Ecclesiastes 5:19 says that God gives us the authority, dominion, and right to enjoy that wealth.

"But Ben," I hear you saying, "I thought you said we weren't supposed to care about success—that we were only supposed to seek God and His righteousness." Yes, our overriding goal in life should be to seek God, not success. But I never said we were not to care about success—only that we are not to allow Success to become our master. We *should* want to succeed in whatever God gives us to do; in fact, success can be a powerful testimony of God to a watching world. "Whatever your hand finds to do," states Ecclesiastes 9:10, "do it with your might." Success should be an outcome of our labor—not an obsession.

The Bible does not teach that poverty is a blessing. Rather, Scripture teaches that poverty is a *curse*—a curse brought about by the fallen state of the world. Isaiah 58:5–7 pictures poverty as a result of human wickedness and oppression, and calls God's people to help set the poor free from their poverty. God's best is for His people to prosper and to use their resources wisely. That's why He said to Israel, "Be strong and of good courage . . . that you may observe to do according to all the law which Moses My servant commanded you; do not turn from it to the right hand or to the left, that you may prosper wherever you go" (Josh. 1:6–7).

"It is good and fitting," wrote Solomon, "for one to eat and drink, and to enjoy the good of all his labor in which he toils under the sun all the days of his life which God gives him; for it is his heritage. As for every man to whom God has given riches and wealth, and given him power to eat of it, to receive his heritage and rejoice in his labor—this is the gift of God" (Eccl. 5:18, 19).

There is nothing inherently wrong with Christians having wealth. However, riches can be a snare for the unwary. It is easy for Christians, once they are well-paid, well-housed, well-fed, and well-clothed to begin to find their security in their wealth instead of in God. That is why God tells us "Beware . . . lest—when you have eaten and are full, and have built beautiful houses and dwell in them . . . you forget the LORD your God" (Deut. 8:11, 12, 14).

Money is a morally neutral commodity, and can be used for good or for evil. Romans 12:8 tells us that there is a spiritual gift of giving, and I believe that this gift is a supernatural, Spirit-endowed ability to generate wealth, coupled with a cheerful, generous, giving attitude. If wealth was an evil thing, there would be no such thing as a spiritual gift of giving! And if Christians did not generate wealth, how could we evangelize, feed the poor, clothe the naked, and care for widows and orphans? What would we give as tithes and offerings to God?

In Deuteronomy 28, God promises to reward, exalt, and pour out blessing after blessing after blessing upon those who are obedient to His Word. This chapter is an incredible array of blessings—blessings which God's people have in store if they will heed and obey the commandments of the Lord. The rest of that same chapter, however, goes on with an awesome list of curses and tribulations that will overtake those who disobey God: poverty, plague, confusion, fear, flight in the face of the enemy, and destruction. Here again, God sets before us a set of choices, and allows us the freedom to use our sovereign decisionability to either obey God or declare war on Him.

God not only gives us permission to be successful, He

actually promises success and material blessing to those who are obedient to His Word.

Third Secret of Success: Define What Success Means to You

In 1923, nine of the world's most powerful and successful businessmen gathered for a high-level meeting at the Edgewater Beach Hotel in Chicago:

1. The president of the largest independent steel company in the country
2. The president of the nation's largest utility
3. The president of the nation's largest gas company
4. The richest grain commodity speculator
5. The president of the New York Stock Exchange
6. A member of the White House cabinet
7. The top Wall Street stock speculator
8. Head of the world's largest industrial cartel
9. President of the Bank of International Settlements

Now, does that sound like a "success summit" or what? By all the standards by which this world measures "success," these men had it all. But did they? Twenty-five years later, the stories of these nine "successful" men had a different ending than anyone would have predicted:

1. Charles Schwab, founder and president of Bethlehem Steel, lived the last five years of his life on borrowed money; he died bankrupt.
2. Utility magnate Samuel Insull fled to a foreign country to escape American justice; he died in poverty and obscurity.
3. Gas company president Howard Hopson ended his days in an insane asylum.
4. Commodities speculator Arthur Cutten died overseas—penniless.

5. Former stock exchange president Richard Whitney spent time in Sing Sing prison.
6. Former cabinet member Albert Fall was also imprisoned.
7. Wall Street wizard Jesse Livermore died by his own hand.
8. Industrial tycoon Ivar Krueger also died by suicide.
9. International financier Leon Fraser also died by suicide.

Each of these "successful" men died an abject failure. So what is success? Success is what you define it to be, according to your beliefs, values, and desires. I have my own definition of success, but my definition of success might not fire your imagination one bit. We each have to decide what constitutes success in our own minds.

The key to arriving at a workable definition of success for your life is in finding the desire that motivates you. If you have a deep desire to see people healed of their diseases, that desire will push you, prod you, and pull you through eight years of medical school, plus another couple years in a grueling, 36-hours-a-day internship. It will give you the stomach for dissecting cadavers and spending your days around diseases and human pain. It can fire your determination to fast, pray, and study the Word so that you can become a healing evangelist, praying on every occasion for the sick. Without true motivation, you'll never achieve it; with motivation, nothing can stop you.

As you define what success means to you, avoid comparing your definition with those of other people. Above all, avoid defining success in terms of money or prestige. I consider Mother Teresa an extremely successful woman. She's not wealthy and it's hard to picture her behind the wheel of a Jaguar—but none of that stuff matters to Mother Teresa. To her, success doesn't mean a thick investment portfolio or being voted Most Admired Woman in the World. Her success is doing the work God gave her to do—ministering to the castoffs in the slums of Calcutta.

Now, what Mother Teresa considers success is probably not success to Madonna or Donald Trump. But at the same time, there are people who look at Madonna and Donald Trump who would say, "That's not success." Many people spend their lives reaching for someone else's definition of success—a palatial home, a Rolls-Royce or a Jaguar in the driveway, a Rolex on the wrist, a Giorgio Armani suit. But when they get to the top rung of the ladder of success, they discover (as Stephen Covey says) that the ladder was "leaning against the wrong wall." These are the "success stories" who end up in detox, on skid row, or dead on the floor with a gun in their hands.

God does not define success for us; He gives us a rainbow of options.

So as you formulate *your* definition of success, remember that He doesn't expect you to thread the needle of His will. God doesn't place you in bondage—He liberates you! "And what does the Lord require of you" asks Micah 6:8, "But to do justly, To love mercy, And to walk humbly with your God?" So, find out what your life's desire is, formulate your definition of success in terms of that desire, proceed along a path that is moral and honoring to God, and *get on with your life!*

"But what if I make a mistake?" you may ask. Well, what if you do? Remember Columbus? He thought he was sailing to China—but he never even got close to China! Now, that's a mistake! But look at what Columbus discovered by mistake: America! So my advice to you is: *Sail on, dude!*

Fourth Secret of Success: Open Your Mind

True story: A famous American writer was taking a bath in his hotel suite when he heard a knock at the door.

He wrapped a towel around his middle and walked out to the door. "Who is it?" he called.

"Telegram!" replied the bellboy on the other side of the door.

"Slide it under the door," said the writer.

"I can't!" returned the bellboy. "It's on a tray!"

Imagine! This bellboy's thinking is so constricted that it doesn't occur to him to take the telegram off the tray and slide it under the door! Now, with this kind of narrow mindset, that bellboy is doomed to never becoming anything but a bellboy—and not even a very good bellboy at that! Yet you and I easily get stuck in that same kind of narrow thinking. Our minds get hemmed in by artificial barriers, like those yellow lines on the highway. We think, "Oh, I can't cross that line. I've never done that before. I've never tried that before. I don't think I could do that."

The reason many of us are hindered or defeated in our own lives is that we are hindered and defeated in our own *minds*. The "minnows" of choice and opportunity are swimming all around us, right within snatching distance —*but we think they are beyond our reach.*

Two friends, both about forty years old, were talking about how their lives had turned out as they reached that zone we call "midlife." One of these men was fairly satisfied with his life, but the other was grumbling and complaining.

"I mean, here I am, forty years old," said the complainer, "and I hate my job, I hate my boss, I hate where I am in life."

"Well," said his buddy, "what would you really like to do?"

"It's crazy. You'll laugh."

"No, I won't. What would you do if you had the chance?"

"I'd be a doctor."

"Well, why don't you become a doctor, if that's what you really want?"

"Man," said the complainer, "it takes ten years of schooling to be a doctor! In ten years, I'll be *fifty years old!*"

His friend paused a moment. "Well, tell me this: How old will you be in ten years if you *don't* become a doctor?"

We make all these excuses for why we "can't" do what we want to do and be what we want to be. "I've got kids; I can't do that." Or, "I've got too many debts, I can't do that." Or, "I'm too old, I can't do that." Or, "I come from this race or that culture, I can't do that." Or, "I'm the wrong gender, I can't do that." Or, "Society has stacked the deck against me, I can't do that." But none of these excuses are valid. Break the imaginary, mental barriers that hinder you, and you will begin to realize some of the amazing potential for achievement and success that God has designed into you.

We can do anything we choose to do. We will have to pay a price, we will have to make sacrifices, we will have to accept consequences, but if we truly open our minds, this fact becomes clear: Our problem is *not* that we "can't" do what we want. Most of us are simply not willing to pay the price or accept the consequences of our choices.

God tells us we can pursue *any* goals, *any* dreams. But to do that, we have to pry open our minds and explore all the endless possibilities that surround us.

Fifth Secret of Success: Set Your Goals

In 1961, President John F. Kennedy declared that America would put a man on the moon before the end of the decade. On July 20, 1969, America did just that. Our nation was successful in the space race because President Kennedy defined a clear, achievable, stated goal.

The same has always been true whenever America needed to achieve a difficult goal. In World War II, the situation was clear: Democracy was threatened around the world, and we had to do something to save it. No one had any doubt about the goal: The total defeat of Nazism, Fascism, and Japanese Imperialism. We knew exactly what we were doing and why we had to do it. We were willing to make the sacrifices necessary to do it. So we sent our men over there to die and we made heroes out of them. On the home front, we did without rubber and nylon and gasoline, we saved dimes, we bought war stamps and bonds, we saved tinfoil. (I don't know what the government did with all that tinfoil, but I sure remember saving it!) As a result, our sacrifices paid off, our objectives were achieved, and America and her allies were successful.

Nations need clear, identifiable, stated goals in order to succeed—and so do people. So how do you formulate goals for your life? You start by setting large, long-range goals: "I want to own my own business," or, "I want to lose fifty pounds," or, "I want to get out of debt." Write that goal on a sheet of paper, then break it down into a series of steps or short-range goals. For example, if your long-range goal is to own your own business, you might set a series of smaller, workable goals such as:

- I will go to the library and the bookstore, and I'll read every book I can on running a business.
- I will arrange a meeting with the Small Business Council so I can get the help and advice I need.
- I will talk to my banker (or father-in-law) to see what kind of funding is available.
- I will get a job in my chosen field for a few months so I can learn the business from the inside out and from the bottom up.

Any big goal in life can be broken down into smaller, less intimidating short-term goals: Reading through the Bible. Getting your college degree. Remodeling your house. Writing that book you've been planning for years. It's simply a matter of cutting up your steak with a steak knife instead of trying to gulp it down whole. Even God broke the task of creation down into six easy steps.

God calls us to think deeply about our lives, to pray and meditate in His Word, to make plans and set goals. Our infallible guidebook for planning and goal-setting is His Word. "This Book of the Law," says God, "shall not depart from your mouth, but you shall meditate in it day and night, that you may observe to do according to all that is written in it. For then you will make your way prosperous, and then you will have good success" (Josh. 1:8).

God is saying, "Think! Meditate! Plan! Set goals! And above all, *heed My Word*! Then you will be successful!" Think of what God is conferring upon you: the rights of a sovereign individual, capable of making your own decisions and setting your own goals, free of any actual physical restraints. You can literally do whatever you want to do. As long as you conform to God's principles, God will stamp His blessing upon your life.

Am I saying this clearly enough? *Whatever you want to do!* Anything? *Yes, ANYTHING!* You can pursue any goals you are willing to accept the consequences for and/or reap the benefits of doing.

5

A SOCIETY ENSLAVED

I was raised in Uvalde, Texas, a sunbaked little town on the Leona River, about eighty miles southwest of San Antonio. In 1955, the year I graduated from high school, something *big*—I mean, *really* big!—happened in our town: They built a brand-new Humble Esso (now Exxon) service station. Now, if you've never lived in a little town like Uvalde, you probably have no idea how much excitement this can generate. I mean, this was a big deal! In those days, they built service stations that were a wonder to behold, with a sleek, modern design, shiny white tile on the outside walls, big, roomy service bays, and gleaming, rounded gas pumps. The people in Uvalde had never seen anything like it before, so many of us went by there every day as this service station was going up.

One day, home for the summer, I went to watch the progress of the construction, I made a strange discovery: There were three doorways in the side of the building. The doors hadn't been hung yet, so I walked up closer, looked inside, and saw that three restrooms were under construction. *Three* rest rooms? Hey, they must have been expecting a lot of people!

A few days later, I came by again and the service station was almost finished. The doors had been hung on the rest rooms, and on each door was a neatly lettered sign: WHITE MEN, WHITE WOMEN, and COLORED.

Well, that was sure not my first encounter with racism, but there was something so officially and institutionally *wrong* about those three signs that my young heart just filled with hurt and rage. I thought, *Man, I'm getting outta here!* So I made up my mind to leave and joined the Air Force. I spent thirteen years in a blue suit, and by the time I left the service in 1968, I was a committed black radical. My brother, who was thirteen years younger than I, was even more radical than I was. I would characterize myself as more of a "moderate radical" and my brother Harvey as a "militant radical." What's the difference? My position was, "Let's demand our civil rights, and if we don't get our rights, let's blow the people up." My brother's position was, "Let's blow 'em up first and negotiate with the survivors."

In 1968, I was ready to enter "the real war," the war for equality and racial justice. I admired the Black Muslims, and would have become one myself, but my appetites got in my way: Muslims don't eat pork, and man, I couldn't see going without ham, pork chops, and bacon! So I was committed to a doctored form of black nationalism without the Muslim religion.

Besides, I agreed with Karl Marx that religion was "the opiate of the people"—especially black people. Religion, in my mind, was a trick designed to focus our eyes on the hereafter. While the rich white people enjoyed their milk and honey right here on earth, poor black people were taught to look forward to streets of gold in heaven. Well, I needed some gold to walk the streets with right now!

As a black radical, I didn't align myself with this group

or that group. Instead, I took a little bit of whatever appealed to me from various movements and the writings of various radical leaders, and I developed a clear strategy.

I saw a lot of radical groups struggling along, espousing what I thought were good ideas but having very little success in achieving meaningful change. I knew that it mattered little how right your cause was if you didn't have the money and power to back it up. So I decided right then and there I was not going to be a footsoldier in a failed movement, carrying out other men's orders, saying, "Ours is not to reason why, ours is but to do and die." No, sir! I was going to be a mover, a shaker, a decision-maker.

My approach had a distinctly capitalist bent to black radicalism. I decided I was going to go back to college, get a degree, get into sales, go into business, and make a lot of money to finance the revolution. I had taken a good hard look at the way business was done in America, and I realized that almost all the CEOs in this country had earned degrees in business administration, then worked in the sales side of the company, and had done very well. Sales was where you made your mark, got noticed, and moved up the line.

So that's where my life was headed when I met Jesus on that General Tire test track.

The Lord Jesus Christ turned me upside down and drained all the bitterness and anger out of my heart. I began to see my life, my heritage, and my country in a different way than I had seen it before. He didn't erase the memory of past injustices from my mind. Instead, He gave me a new perspective on all the hurts that had been inflicted on me, and the four hundred years of injustice and horror that had been imposed on black people in general.

I look around at the angry, bitter young blacks today and I see the rage of my own youth. It grieves me, because I know how that rage feels, I know how self-destructive it is—and I also know there is a better way. American blacks—and indeed many people in America today—are being taught that there is no more opportunity for them in America, that racism, sexism, and more has locked them out of the American dream, that their only hope for survival is government programs, government housing, or a government check.

At the same time, it should be noted that the black culture is not the welfare-addicted, solidly liberal voting bloc that the media portrays it to be. The American work ethic is strongest in the (over-forty) segment of the African-American community. One of the reasons black people over forty appreciate the benefits and opportunities of America is that we remember when we didn't have them. I can distinctly remember a time, not so long ago, when I couldn't just walk into any restaurant I wanted or use any washroom I wanted to, get or even apply for any job I was qualified to do.

So when we talk about issues such as sovereignty, choice, freedom, and responsibility, we're talking about something that is intensely, personally real to me. It is very real to a lot of black people. It breaks our hearts to see a younger generation of blacks growing up who are willing to hand over their sovereign responsibility and decisionability to drug dealers or a paternalistic government.

Failure on a Massive Scale

One morning a few years ago, my mother was in the front yard of her home, doing some gardening or rosebush trimming or whatnot, when a neighbor lady—we'll call her Miss Martinez—came over from across the street for a chat. Miss Martinez was a young single mother with several children. "Oh, Mrs. Kinchlow," said Miss Martinez, "I just don't know how I'm going to make it this month!"

My mother glanced across the street to Miss Martinez's yard, where the young woman's children were playing—and she remembered what it was like when she was Miss Martinez's age, trying to make ends meet and raise two boys on my father's wages. "I know it's hard," my mother agreed.

"They just oughta give us more money!" Miss Martinez said bitterly.

"*Who* ought to give you more money?"

"The government! They don't give us hardly enough to live like decent folk! I only get six hundred a month from AFDC and two hundred a month in food stamps. How's a person supposed to live on that?"

"You're also on WIC, aren't you? And the government pays your rent and your utilities?"

"Yes—But it's just not enough. I mean, what am I gonna do? I'm almost out of diapers for my babies, and I don't have enough money to go down to the store and buy even one box of Pampers!"

"Why don't you just buy cloth diapers and wash them?"

"Well, why don't they just give me more money so I can buy Pampers?"

"Wait a minute!" said my mother. "The way they give you more money is to take money from my husband. He's out there working every day and you aren't working—not even washing out a few cloth diapers to make ends meet. And you're telling me that you want the government to take *more* money out of my husband's pocket to give to you so you don't have to wash a few stinky diapers?"

"Well," said Miss Martinez, taken aback. "I just want them to give me more money. The government has all that money, and if the government runs out of money, it can just print some more, right? All I want is for the government to give me enough money so that I can go buy some Pampers!"

Miss Martinez is like a lot of people who are locked into these so-called "entitlements"—welfare, Medicaid, and other entrenched government programs. She doesn't have the foggiest idea of how these "entitlement" programs are funded, who pays for them, or how destructive these programs are to herself and her children. The devastating legacy of the American welfare state is that it has left people like Miss Martinez completely in the dark about how this country works, how wealth is generated, how to access the vast opportunities for advancement in this country, and how to build a better life for themselves and the next generation.

How did we get into this mess?

It all started with good intentions. Although the earliest experiments with welfare state programs actually go back to the late 1800s, the rise of the modern welfare state began with the misery of the Great Depression. The American people, being a compassionate people, wanted to alleviate the hardships of the poor, the unemployed, the disabled, the elderly, and those who lacked adequate medical care. The original idea behind government social spending was to care for the relatively few people in this country who couldn't fend for themselves, while giving a temporary hand to those who were down on their luck. Good goals! But no one, back in the 1930s and 1940s, foresaw what would result from these policies some fifty or sixty years later:

- Today there are over 100 overlapping "giveaway" programs administered by over a dozen different federal agencies: Aid to Families with Dependent Children (AFDC); Supplemental Security Income (SSI); Emergency Assistance (EA); General Assistance (GA); Medicaid; food stamps; public and subsidized housing; the school lunch program; the Supplemental Food Program for Women, Infants, and Children (WIC); and the Low-Income Energy Assistance program; job-training and job-search programs; federally funded day-care centers, family planning centers, and drug and alcohol rehab centers.

- Nearly one of every seven American children is in a family receiving federally funded Aid to Families with Dependent Children.
- Nearly 20 percent of all children born in the late 1960s have spent at least one year on welfare (that figure skyrockets to more than 70 percent for African-American children).
- The annual welfare budget now tops $300 billion.
- Some five million American households are now on welfare.

Now, if you crunch those numbers, a really interesting fact emerges. By dividing the $300 billion welfare budget by five million families, you get a figure of *$60,000 per family*! Clearly, if every poor family received $60,000 a year, they wouldn't be poor anymore. Obviously, welfare families don't get anything like $60,000 a year, even when you add up all the food, health care, rent subsidies, and every other form of government assistance they receive. (The actual figure, as of 1994, was $5,790 received per poor person, or $20,163 per family below the poverty level.) Where does all the rest of that money go? It goes to administrative overhead! It pays bureaucrats and buys office equipment and prints government forms. In fact, the U.S. welfare system operates with a *74 percent overhead*, which means that it costs the government *four dollars* just to give away *one dollar*! (*Reader's Digest*, March 1995).

Now, it would be bad enough if our welfare system were "only" wasteful. But the problem goes beyond waste, beyond fraud, and beyond bureaucratic boondoggle. Welfare, when you get right down to it, is mean and destructive! It creates dependence, it kills individual initiative, it breaks down families, it generates failure on a massive scale. In short, it *undermines the sovereignty* of the people it is supposed to help, and keeps them from realizing their magnificent, God-given potential!

What Gets Rewarded Gets Done

Suppose you are a young man, about nineteen years old, and an old gent comes up to you and says, "I'm your rich relative. I have more money than you can count, and I will pay for every baby you can make by as many different women as you can."

"Really?" you say. "What's the catch?"

"No catch. All you have to do is make the babies, and I will support them until they are eighteen years of age. My only requirement is that you never live with any of those women, and you never contribute a dime of support to any of those babies. In fact, if you try and take responsibility, I won't help you. But as long as you don't lift a finger to help that child, I will feed him, clothe him, house him, and give him full health care until he is eighteen."

"How many times can I do that?"

"As often as you want."

"How many women?"

"As many as you can. Now, tell me—how many babies could you make?"

You might think, "That's just plain ridiculous, Ben! No one would make a stupid offer like that!"

Oh, really? That promise is made to thousands of young men every day in this country. That rich relative is Uncle Sam, and the promise is welfare. And there's more:

- "We'll give you so much cash assistance, food assistance, medical assistance, and housing assistance that you can't afford to take an entry-level job to get off welfare."
- "If you try to get a job or any other additional help, we'll cut off all your assistance."
- "If you don't qualify for assistance, we'll show you how to lie so that you can get your slice of the welfare 'entitlement' pie."
- "If you are addicted to drugs and alcohol, we will declare you disabled and give you a disability check every month to enable your addiction and help you pay for your drugs."

The result of these policies has been a rise in teenage pregnancy, illegitimacy, and single-parent families, and a spiraling breakdown of the American family. We have actually created *financial rewards* for teenage pregnancy, illegitimacy, and broken families! The principle is clear: *Whatever gets rewarded gets done.*

In his 1965 State of the Union speech, President Lyndon B. Johnson launched his so-called "Great Society," an agenda of welfare state programs which included Medicare and the Department of Housing and Urban Development. That year, the divorce rate was only 10 divorces per 1,000 marriages. The illegitimacy rate was only 5 percent on average—2 percent among whites and 22 percent among blacks. Only 13 percent of children lived in one-parent households.

By 1979, the divorce rate had increased 130 percent, to 23 divorces per year per 1,000 marriages. By 1991, the illegitimacy rate had climbed to 30 percent—22 percent among whites, 68 percent among blacks; that same year, fully 30 percent of all children lived in one-parent households (19 percent of white kids, 31 percent of Latino kids, and 49 percent of black kids) ("Nightline," September 1994).

I'm convinced there is a straight-line correlation between the disintegration of the American family, the removal of God from the public square, and the rise of the American welfare state. If you wanted to deliberately kill the soul and values of a nation, if you wanted to destroy the initiative of the individual, if you wanted to undermine the sovereignty of human beings, you could not come up with a more diabolical instrument of destruction than the welfare state. It totally flies in the face of the instinctive drives that God built into human beings.

God never intended for this wonderful, creative, intelligent, sovereign human race, made in His own image and likeness, to become wards of the state. He never intended that human beings should hand their sovereignty and decisionability over to some "Big Brother." The welfare state doesn't just take away people's right to fail; it takes away their right to make intelligent choices and their right to succeed. A free society is made up of individuals who are self-directed, accountable, and responsible for their own lives. A society of dependents is a society *enslaved*— and a society doomed to collapse. The welfare state didn't work in the Soviet Union, and it is not working in America.

Since Lyndon Johnson declared a "war on poverty" in the 1960s, we have spent $5.3 trillion on anti-poverty programs (a trillion is a *thousand billion*). Now, you would think we could accomplish an awful lot with more than *five thousand billion dollars*. I mean, by now that "war on poverty" should have been won, right? But the fact is, poverty is winning the war. Despite all the money we have thrown at the problem, the underclass has been steadily growing, not shrinking, over the past thirty years.

What do the proponents of the welfare state have to say about this? They say we aren't spending enough! They say we aren't compassionate enough! They say we need to give away *more* money! It seems to me that if you keep doing what you've been doing, you'll keep getting what you've been getting. These "solutions" have only made the problem worse, not better. Instead of spending more, perhaps we should spend less—a lot less.

"Whoa, there, Ben!" you might say. "Where's your Christian compassion?"

Yes, I want to see our society express genuine compassion for the poor. But true "compassion" cannot be administered by a government agency. A bureaucrat can't dispense compassion from a government handbook or checkbook. Compassion comes from the heart, not from a government computer. If the job of ministering to the needy was put back in the hands of truly charitable people and agencies, the needs of all the *truly* needy could be met—privately and locally.

The Entitlement Mentality

You know the story: On March 3, 1991, Rodney Glen King led officers of the Los Angeles Police Department and the California Highway Patrol on a high-speed chase. He was stopped and "beaten" by police batons while resisting arrest. The "beating" was captured on videotape, and the officers were put on trial for police brutality. When those officers were acquitted by a mostly white jury on April 30, 1992, the city of Los Angeles was rocked by five days of rioting, arson, and looting.

Now here's a piece of the story that perhaps you *didn't* know: During those riots, more than seven thousand guns disappeared from various pawnshops and gun shops around L.A. Where are those guns now? They're somewhere in the 'hood, my friend. My guess is that this isn't the last we've heard of those seven thousand guns. When will those guns come out again in force?

The *next* L.A. riot could be over welfare reform.

The problem is that all too many people feel that a check from the government is their right. Welfare is not just some temporary measure to get them through a stretch of hard times. It's their entitlement for life! Cut off that check, and you are throwing down a personal affront. "That's my money," they say—because that's exactly what the government has been telling them for as long as two, three, four, or five generations. If you tell them you are going to take that check away, what do you think they will do?

The national media and the liberal leadership in this country have persistently hammered into minority people the idea that this country is responsible for their problems. They preach the idea that minorities are owed something from the government—a check, a program, a service—and that anyone who would take those government benefits from them is a "racist." People in the welfare-dependent underclass have lived with these attitudes for so long, they don't have anything else to compare it to. To them, the idea that they can't make it without government benefits is just a given. It doesn't even occur to them to access the benefits of the American system.

At the same time, you see refugees and immigrants streaming into this country from Asia, Eastern Europe, Latin America, and the Caribbean, and these immigrants are working hard, taking the jobs that native-born Americans refuse to take, starting their own businesses, and reaping the benefits of the opportunities of this country.

I know of one family in my own community in Virginia who came here as refugees from Cuba. When they arrived, they had nothing. The entire family lived in one or two rooms. They took any jobs they could get, they put their kids in school, they started a janitorial business and worked long, hard hours. Today they are worth over a million dollars, they own a big house in a nice part of town, and their kids are studying and preparing for business and professional careers. There are literally thousands of such stories taking place across America every day, and when you hear one of those stories you wonder, "What about the people who live here?"

There are people who live here all their lives, yet never understand the opportunities they have! They go to American schools, they understand the laws and customs, they know the language—yet they end up living in government housing, cashing government checks, and wasting their lives watching TV all day. Why? Because they've been indoctrinated into this nonsense that the country "owes" them something, that they are "entitled" to a living without ever having their dignity demeaned by an entry-level "McJob".

As I write these words, there is a lot of talk from both political parties, from liberals and conservatives, about overhauling "the welfare mess" and "ending welfare as we know it." Despite all the talk, I've seen very little substantive action. But assuming something really does get done, and welfare can be effectively overhauled or ended, we still have a big job to do.

To the Nth Generation

According to the statistics, a child raised on welfare is 300 percent more likely to become welfare-dependent in adulthood than other children. Generation by generation, those on welfare come to feel less and less guilty about what they are doing, while gradually learning to view welfare as their entitlement. Here we see the mechanism of Exodus 34:7 at work: "The iniquity of the fathers [is visited] upon the children and the children's children to the third and the fourth generation." Values of hard work, responsibility, and sovereign decisionability must be consciously, carefully passed from one generation to the next, through both word and example. Values disintegrate if they are not carefully preserved. That is why God says,

> And these words which I command you today shall be in your heart. You shall teach them diligently to your children, and shall talk of them when you sit in your house, when you walk by the way, when you lie down, and when you rise up (Deut. 6:6–7.)

Over the generations, as the strength of the family line deteriorates, one generation may wake up and say, "What are we doing? Why are we living like this?" Multigenerational decline is reversible—but why put the generations through all that pain? The Gospel of Jesus Christ has the power to *lift* people—not only out of sin, but out of their apathy, out of their poverty, out of their economic bondage, and out of the deception of the entitlement mentality!

The best hope, perhaps the only hope, of reversing America's steeply tilting trend toward economic dependency, bondage, and insolvency is the lifting power of the Gospel. Unless great numbers of people in the underclass begin to grasp the fact of their own sovereignty and of God's ability to lift them out of the pain of their poverty, the nation is headed either for economic collapse or social disintegration.

In the next chapter, we will see that our American society was originally envisioned as *a society of sovereigns,* and we will see the amazing future this country could still have ahead of her if that vision could be recaptured.

6

A SOCIETY OF SOVEREIGNS

It was near the end of a hot summer day in Fresno, California, in 1992. Tragically, it would be the last day of 18-year-old Kimber Reynolds' life.

Kimber and a male friend, also 18 years old, had just had dinner together at the Daily Planet, a trendy uptown restaurant. They were crossing the sidewalk to Kimber's car, which was parked on the street. Kimber let her friend in on the passenger side and then walked around to the driver's side and opened the door to get in.

Just then she heard the roar of a motorcycle and the squeal of rubber. Startled, she turned and found herself pinned against the open door of her car by a motorcycle. On the motorcycle were two men. One of them lunged for her purse. "No!" she shouted, yanking her purse back. "You're not taking my purse!"

One of the men on the cycle pulled out a .357 Magnum and shoved it up against Kimber's ear. What Kimber didn't know is that these two guys were not just a couple of ordinary punks; they were hardened, violent repeat offenders. The cycle they were riding was stolen, and they had made a career of robbing, raping, and killing. The gunman didn't offer her a "gimme-the-purse-or-I'll-shoot" option. He just pulled the trigger, and Kimber dropped to the pavement. Then he and his buddy roared off with Kimber's purse.

Over the next few hours, the young woman's parents—photographer Mike Reynolds and his wife, Sharon—lived through any parent's worst nightmare: They watched helplessly as their daughter's life ebbed away. There at Kimber's bedside, Mike Reynolds made a pledge to his daughter. "I promise you," he told her, "I'll do everything in my power to keep this from happening to another person, another daughter, another parent." A little after midnight, Kimber was pronounced dead.

In the next few weeks, Kimber's killers were brought to justice. One was killed in a shootout with police while resisting arrest; the other was tried, convicted, and sentenced to nine years (he will probably serve half of his sentence, about four and a half years). But that was not the end of the story for Mike Reynolds. Not by a long shot.

Reynolds began by holding a number of backyard barbeques, inviting state legislators, judges, and local news personalities to attend. Out of those backyard meetings came an idea which has since become a grassroots revolution. Someone in those meetings came up with a label which has since become a national slogan: "Three Strikes and You're Out!" The basic concept is that if a person has committed a violent felony, then that offense becomes a "strike." We now know what this person is capable of, so if he commits a second felony, violent or not, we can crank up the punishment and double the sentence. Three felonies? He gets the max. Under Three Strikes, we don't have to let a criminal go out and kill again before we put him away; society takes the offensive and puts bad guys out of business *before* they kill again.

Does Three Strikes work? In the first year since it became law in California, the murder rate dropped by 21 percent in Los Angeles. Statewide, the crime rate in almost all categories dropped dramatically, and the increase in the incarceration rate slowed, up only 4.5 percent in 1994 versus 17.7 percent in 1993. The number of inbound felons (parolees from other states requesting transfers into California) dropped virtually to nothing—suddenly, criminals lost all interest in moving to a Three Strikes state! Lawmakers had been planning to add 20 new prisons to the penal system by the year 2000, but the sudden decline in the crime rate has caused 6 of those prison-building projects to be canceled. Handgun sales dropped by 8 percent in 1994—the first decline in ten years, and a sign that people in the state feel less of a sense of urgency about defending themselves and their families. (Story and statistics courtesy of Mike Reynolds.)

Yes, I think we can safely say that Three Strikes has had an impact.

Human society was designed by God to be a society of self-governing, self-directed sovereigns. Unfortunately, because of human sin, there are some in society who cannot refrain from violating the sovereignty of their fellow human beings. They steal, they rape, they murder, they commit various sorts of crimes against their fellow sovereigns. Those who demonstrate an inability to respect the sovereignty of others, committing crime after crime, must be taken out of society and put someplace where they can do no more harm. "Three Strikes" legislation is one way to do this, and Mike Reynolds is to be commended for the way he has taken the pain of his own personal tragedy, and transformed it into legislation to protect the lives and property of millions of other people.

"Three Strikes" legislation has been criticized by some

in government and in the media. They point to the fact that some criminals have been sentenced to life in prison for stealing a lawn mower out of someone's garage or, in one case, for stealing a few slices of pizza! The liberals say that these penalties don't fit the crime. The fact is, however, that most of these criminals were previously convicted of violent crimes, and after serving time for those crimes, and even knowing that the new "Three Strikes" law placed their freedom in jeopardy, they went back into society and continued to commit crimes. What they were saying by these actions is: "Of my own free will, I reject the privilege of living in a self-governing society, and I accept the risk that, if caught and convicted, I may spend the rest of my natural life in prison. That is my sovereign choice."

Life is a series of choices. If you make bad decisions, you have to pay the consequences. The reason people get into prison in the first place is that they have made some bad decisions. Now, some of these people spend their time in prison reconsidering the course of their lives and making constructive changes in their behavior. Others learn nothing from their experience except how to be better criminals. Still others actually seem to prefer life behind bars—perhaps because there are fewer decisions to make. In prison, you have someone telling you when to get up, when to go out, when to exercise, when to eat, when to shower, and when to go to bed. Those who can't handle the "pressure" of being a responsible, self-directed sovereign will sometimes commit a crime just to get rearrested, trading in their freedom for a structured life without any vexing decisions to make.

In the long and heated debate over crime and punishment in this country, one thing has gotten lost: why penitentiaries were established in the first place. Some people think the reason we have prisons is to rehabilitate criminals. If rehabilitation takes place, that's fine—but that's not why penitentiaries were established. Some think the reason we have prisons is to punish wrongdoers, to exact society's vengeance against those who commit offenses. Again, that view misses the point of why prisons were originally established.

Penitentiaries were predicated upon the concept that *sovereign human beings have a right to exist in society, free from threats to their person and property.* People who cannot govern their actions and respect the sovereignty of others do not have the right to walk about freely in a society of self-governing sovereigns. Those who violate the laws of man—which, in the beginning, were based on the laws of God in the Bible—forfeit their rights and their status as sovereign, self-governing individuals.

What was the original basis for the punishment of crime? The God-given sovereignty of human beings, made in His image and likeness. God originally established a plan for law and order which divided crimes into two broad categories—capital crimes and property crimes.

Capital crimes are those involving a violation of the sovereignty of another human being: kidnapping, rape, or murder. The principle was set down by God in Genesis 9:6—"Whoever sheds man's blood, by man his blood shall be shed; *for in the image of God He made man.*" The punishment for willful violation of the sovereignty of others is clear, unappealable, nonnegotiable: death. For when you violate another person's sovereignty, you violate the image and likeness of God which was stamped upon that person at creation—and you must pay with your life.

Property crimes—burglary, robbery, theft, and the like —are adjudicated very simply: A thief, says Proverbs 6:31, "must restore sevenfold." You steal a dollar, you pay back seven dollars. You steal a thousand dollars, you pay back seven thousand. If you must take an extra job or sell all your possessions, you do it. If you have to pay in installments while doing time at hard labor, you do it. That's your debt, no two ways about it. When you are released again to society, everyone knows you are a thief, and they watch you like a hawk. Punishment is designed to ensure that everyone in society knows that *crime doesn't pay*.

Those who can't keep themselves from violating the sovereignty and the property of others have to be isolated from society. If you want to be "compassionate" and give a thief two or three strikes to get serious about the direction of his life, and to feel the ratcheting up of the penalties for stealing with each successive strike, that's O.K. On strike three, you're out, buddy. You knew what the penalties were, you made your choice, you did the crime, now you do the time. End of story.

You take someone's life, then forget about three strikes. You only get one time at bat, then you're out of the game —for good. Why? Because "in the image of God He made man."

Some might say, "But that's barbaric!" No, that's not barbaric. It's barbaric to live in a fear-ridden society where criminals have no dread of the law. There is nothing barbaric about a murderer paying for his crime with his life, because *nobody has to commit a crime*. All you have to do to avoid the death penalty is to respect the sovereignty of others. If you never kill another human being, the death penalty holds no terror for you.

Once you see society as a community of sovereigns, your understanding of crime is transformed. A crime is not just a game of cops and robbers. A crime is *an act of war* committed by one sovereign against another sovereign. You cannot declare war against another sovereign unless you are prepared to accept the consequences and absorb the retaliation your act of war deserves.

We are all sovereign individuals in the sight of God, and our laws, our social behavior, and our social structure should reflect that fact.

Government of the Sovereigns, by the Sovereigns, for the Sovereigns

The very uniqueness of our American way of life lies in its celebration of the sovereignty of the individual. Ours is strictly a government *of* the people, *by* the people, and *for* the people.

Under a monarchy, the king or queen is sovereign, not the individual. In totalitarian societies, the dictator is sovereign, not the individual. In socialist and communist societies, the state is sovereign, not the individual. But in a representative democracy, such as we have, the individual has the ascendancy, not the government. That is why the Bill of Rights was appended to the Constitution: The framers of the Constitution understood that the sovereignty of the people had to be respected and defended in the foundational document of this radical new society.

Over the years, however, we have drifted away from an understanding of the sovereignty of the people. We have veered away from the concept of the individual as the repository of rights and responsibilities in a free society. Instead, we have come to view certain groups as having sovereign rights. The founding fathers would have been horrified to see the rights of a sovereign individual abridged in the name of "affirmative action."

We have also drifted away from an understanding of where our rights descend from. The writers of the Declaration of Independence knew: "We hold these truths to be self-evident, that all men are created equal, *that they are endowed by their Creator with certain unalienable Rights*, that among these are Life, Liberty, and the pursuit of Happiness." Our rights do not come from the Constitution. They don't come from the government. They come only, expressly, and directly from God, the Creator of the universe! Because the Creator has created us in His own image, no human being has the right to rule another human being without his express written consent. That is why the Declaration goes on to say that governments "[derive] their just powers from the consent of the governed." That is why those who work in the government are called "public servants," not masters.

The founding fathers wrote the Declaration of Independence, established the Constitution, amended it with the Bill of Rights—all in order to ensure that this society of sovereign individuals, designed by God to be free and self-directed, would never be under the heel of some master or tyrant. Our government was constructed in such a way that the sovereign people would willingly and voluntarily surrender a limited measure of their sovereignty to their representatives, who would then govern wisely and responsively, in accordance with the wishes of the governed.

This was something totally new and radical! Where did this innovative view of government come from? It emerged in the Constitutional Convention in Philadelphia, which convened in May 1787. There, representatives of twelve states (all but Rhode Island) met to design a new government, built upon the foundation of a new Constitution. Present at the Convention were such luminaries as George Washington, Alexander Hamilton, James Madison, John Jay, and 81-year-old elder statesman Benjamin Franklin.

From the very beginning, the Convention was torn by conflict and bickering. The biggest bone of contention was an argument over legislative power: The larger, more populous states wanted states' representation in the federal government to be based on population; the smaller states wanted every state to have the same number of representatives. Arguments, shouting, and division were common as the Convention dragged through the hot, muggy Philadelphia summer. Many of the delegates became so disgusted they packed up and went home.

Just as the Convention appeared to be on the verge of collapse, white-haired, timeworn Ben Franklin rose to his feet and leaned on his cane for support. All eyes turned his way.

Franklin made a motion that the Convention recess for prayer, and that, henceforth, every future session be opened with prayer. Franklin's motion was adopted, and the delegates withdrew to commit themselves to God's leadership. They prayed, they fasted, they went to church, they read the Scriptures, they sought the face of God for the direction this newborn nation should take. After the weekend, when the delegates reassembled, they opened their first session with prayer. Immediately, everyone present noted that an amazing change had transpired within the Convention hall. Many delegates later made note of this change in their personal journals.

Soon, a compromise emerged to resolve the main sticking point of the Convention: the so-called "Great Compromise" which produced a legislature comprised of two houses, a Senate giving each state equal representation and a House of Representatives giving each state proportional representation based on population. After this breakthrough, most of the other points of conflict seemed to resolve themselves without effort. Within days, the delegates finished hammering together the greatest document ever devised to protect the rights of individuals: the Constitution of the United States of America.

As a result of the lesson learned at the Constitutional Convention of 1787, our nation chose to open each session of the House and Senate with prayer. To this day, government-paid chaplains lead both houses in prayer before the business of state is conducted. And even the Supreme Court precedes its deliberations with the pronouncement, "Oyez, oyez, the Supreme Court is now in session, God bless this honorable court." The framers of our Constitution had experienced firsthand the incredible power of absolute reliance on God to make wise decisions. They were determined, right from the start, that this nation would be "one nation under God."

I am convinced that America is God's idea. Historically, this nation has been God's demonstration to a watching world of exactly what can happen when His presence and His principles are instilled into a nontheistic society. America was designed by God to show that His principles are so effective, so universal, and so transcendent that you can successfully operate any enterprise upon them without specifically articulating, "Thus sayeth the Lord."

America was not the first demonstration of these principles. Thousands of years earlier, God had already demonstrated what happens when His presence and principles are followed by a theistic society—a society organized around and ruled by God—because that is what ancient Israel was. Even though Israel demanded and received a king in the days of Saul (see 1 Samuel 11), Israel was still a theocracy, ruled by God through the mediation of prophets, priests, judges, and kings. The history of Israel also served as a demonstration of what happens when God and His principles are *abandoned*: It was Israel's defection from God that immediately preceded the ruin of the nation of Israel and the dispersion of its people across the world.

Despite such mottoes as "one nation under God" and "in God we trust," the United States has never been a theocracy. While we have historically acknowledged God's divine guidance and protection over our nation, we have also carefully guarded the principle of religious pluralism contained in the First Amendment to the Constitution. All the various references to God in the Declaration of Independence and other documents of our founding fathers are of a nonsectarian nature. Even so, the foundational concept of America has been proven true beyond any shadow of a doubt: a society of free, sovereign, self-directed individuals has the inherent ability to create a virtual "paradise on earth" by living in accordance with the principles of God.

Belief in God and an understanding of Scripture were an integral part of the founding of our nation. Even the three branches of our government—the judicial, the legislative, and the executive branches—were originally patterned by the founding fathers after the government of God, as described in the Old Testament:

> For the LORD is our Judge,
> The LORD is our Lawgiver,
> The LORD is our King;
> He will save us (Isa. 33:22).

John Adams, the second president of the United States, said, "Our Constitution was made only for a moral and religious people. It is wholly inadequate to the government of any other." And George Washington, in his farewell address of 1796, observed, "Of all the dispositions and habits which lead to political prosperity, religion and morality are indispensable supports."

The miracle that is America could only take place if the American people were (1) free to govern themselves, and (2) responsible enough to govern themselves wisely and justly. When a people are not allowed to govern themselves at all, then there is only one way to hold that society together—the same power that kept the Soviet Union from collapsing for over seventy years: secret police and brute force. Yet, if a people are given freedom, but do not exercise it wisely and justly, if they use their freedom as a license for immorality or to vote themselves truckloads of goodies from the public treasury, then collapse and bondage are just around the corner.

Even though the founding fathers were careful to avoid establishing a state religion as existed in England, they still acknowledged the importance of strong moral and religious character in those who would lead the country. In the constitution of each of the thirteen original colonies, there was a provision regarding the qualifications for public office which stated that a public servant must be a person who believes in a transcendent God who judges in the world to come. Atheists and agnostics were precluded from office. Why? The founders of the country were saying, in effect, "We want people in our government to have a conscience and a respect for the sovereignty of the people they serve. We want public servants who believe in a God of judgment, a God who punishes the guilty, a God who balances the scales of justice in this life and in the life to come." They understood that people of religious and moral conviction were less likely to steal and to abuse their power in office. Public servants were expected to perform their present service in light of future judgment.

The American experiment was an amazing concept. There had been governments before—among the Babylonians, the Greeks, the Romans, and the Europeans— where certain classes of nobility or landowners had been given a measure of self-determination. But America was the first example in human history of a nation where all the people were given the right to vote, to elect representatives, and to decide their own political fate. The framers of the Constitution—after setting aside time for prayer and fasting—came to a recognition of the greatness and sovereignty of human beings, made in the image of God. And these early American leaders trusted the sovereign American people with their own destiny.

There was only one previous time in human history when the people at large were trusted with their own destiny: when God placed human beings in the Garden of Eden and said, "Here are your choices." The American Declaration of Independence and the U.S. Constitution accomplish something very much like what God Himself designed for us in the beginning: the freedom to enjoy our God-given life, liberty, and pursuit of happiness—and the responsibility to choose our own destiny.

Historically, this amazing society of sovereigns has succeeded in making very good collective choices, and our nation has prospered accordingly. We have tended to be a moral and religiously devout people. We made a choice to end slavery, even at the cost of a bloody civil war. Again and again, we have chosen to side with less powerful nations when they have been attacked by aggressors. We have opened our doors to immigrants and refugees. We have worked toward building a just society, free of class exploitation and racial hatred. We have reached out with the hand of charity to people who were hurting or down on their luck.

But in recent years, we have strayed from our earlier wisdom. We have allowed millions of innocent babies to be slaughtered in the name of "choice." We have demanded the "freedom" to engage in any behavior we want, regardless of consequences—and our nation is being ravaged by plagues, abortions, and teenage pregnancies. Instead of teaching our children to be pure, we tell them to "be careful." As a result, we are seeing exactly what happened in the Garden of Eden: Wickedness has come in to poison the land, and our Eden is becoming a cesspool.

Two men who were raised in the same poor neighborhood, living within a block of each other. Both had been abandoned by their fathers and raised by drug-addicted, neglectful, abusive mothers. Both had seen many muggings and shootings during their childhood and adolescence. One of these men worked hard to overcome the poverty, abuse, and pain of his early years, applied himself to his studies, worked his way through college and seminary, and became a minister. The other got involved with gangs, and eventually ended up on death row.

A newspaper reporter heard about these two men who had come from such similar beginnings, yet took such different paths. The reporter decided to write a story paralleling these two lives. When he interviewed the minister, he asked, "Given the kind of background you come from, how do you account for the way your life has turned out?"

"Look at the home I came from," said the minister. "The neglect, the beatings, the poverty. I mean, I had to fight against it and overcome it, or it would have destroyed me. With the background I came from, how else could I have turned out?"

The reporter later put the same question to the man on death row: "How do you account for the way your life has turned out?"

"Look at the home I came from," the condemned prisoner replied bitterly. "Look at the way I was treated—beaten, neglected, and all. I *had* to become the meanest so-and-so on the block in order to survive! With the background I came from, how else could I have turned out?"

What spelled the difference between these two men? Only one thing: the sovereign choices they made. We are not ruled by external stimuli. We are not merely a product of our conditioning. Whatever our background, whatever we have gone through, we still have the power to make choices.

Many people—particularly the elitists of the left—do not believe people have the capacity to make their own choices. When you get right down to it, they really don't like people. They are condescending and paternalistic, saying, "We know what is best for you. Let us make the decisions for your life. If we leave it up to you, you'll mess it all up. Let us take care of you. Hand your sovereignty over to us, put us in charge, and we'll make sure you don't have to make any more decisions in life. We, the elitists of the state, will be your sovereigns."

And this is how, in a totalitarian state, the government takes the place of God over people who were intended, by God, to be sovereign.

Paradise Lost

You've seen the images of grinding poverty in Central and South America—the naked, undernourished children with vacant eyes, standing beside cardboard shanties; the villages without running water; the streets with raw sewage trickling down the gutters; the revolutions and political murders and social instability; the "banana republics" where governments change hands with disturbing frequency. Why are these countries so poor and so troubled, when just a few hundred miles to the north is the richest nation on the planet? Is it because the United States is rich in raw materials and natural resources, while Central and South America are naturally poor?

Absolutely not! In fact, these nations south of our borders actually possess far greater resources than we do. The reason North America is so rich and Central and South America are so poor can be found in the very different histories of these two regions: The southern Europeans (mostly Spaniards) who emigrated to Central and South America came seeking gold. The northern Europeans who emigrated to North America came seeking God. The Spaniards wanted wealth; the northern Europeans wanted religious freedom. The Spaniards found their gold in South America; the northern Europeans found their God in North America.

Who, ultimately, became rich? The answer is obvious.

In North America, the settlers from northern Europe acknowledged and respected man's God-given sovereignty, and the result was the United States of America. In Central and South America, though the settlers brought their religion with them, the sovereignty of man was not respected. The people were subjugated, and religion became a tool to aid in that subjugation. As a result, many of these Latin American countries tend to be hostile to the Gospel of Jesus Christ.

Most Latin American countries are economically closed societies, with a thin crust of very rich people at the top and great masses of poor people at the bottom—with no middle class, and no access points to the extreme wealth at the top. Wealth and position are passed down from generation to generation, and the only way you can access wealth or power in large parts of Latin America is to join a revolutionary movement, overthrow the government, and then you go in, steal it, and become the new upper crust —at least until the next revolution! The discontent bred by the spiritual, material, and physical hunger in Latin America have made these countries ripe for revolution, Marxism, and dictatorship.

In America, however, it is completely the other way around: We have a huge middle class, with a thin crust of rich people on the top and another thin crust on the bottom. Best of all, the doorway is always open for people to move from one class to another. Many people start at the bottom and make their way right to the top. Millionaires are made in America every single day—but not in Latin America.

We call the wide-open opportunity in this country *the American dream*. It is that guarantee we find in the Declaration of Independence which says that we are endowed by God with certain inalienable rights, including the right to life, the right to liberty, and the right to pursue happiness. In other words, we have a sovereign, God-given right to live freely and to pursue whatever course of action will bring us happiness, so long as we don't infringe on the rights of the sovereign neighbor right next to us. It doesn't guarantee we will be happy—only that we can pursue happiness. The founding fathers knew: Happiness is not an end in itself, it is a by-product of doing something worthwhile and pursuing something meaningful and significant. So they gave us the freedom to dream our dreams, pursue worthwhile goals, and achieve happiness.

This unquenchable American dream, this confident, almost prideful "We can!" spirit, is the reason America acquired the Louisiana Purchase, conquered the Rockies, spread down the Mississippi, up the Missouri, out the Ohio, across the plains, to the coast of California, from sea to shining sea! There was nobody to say, "You can't."

Not that American history was without its injustices. I once saw a cartoon depicting two kids standing on a street corner. One says to the other, "Do you want to play cops and alleged perpetrators or cowboys and Native Americans?" Now, I don't agree with all the latest politically correct terminology, but as we examine the history of the early American expansion, we have to acknowledge that many people of various races were poorly treated during the early growth and development of our nation. The growth of the American nation could have easily taken place without such atrocities against American Indians as the Wounded Knee Massacre and the Cherokee Trail of Tears. The modern multicultural movement has gotten a lot of things wrong, but one thing the multiculturalists are correct about is the fact that there were already people here when the first European settlers waded ashore. If the God-given sovereignty of the first Americans had been respected from the beginning, hundreds of heartbreaking tragedies in our nation's history could have been avoided.

Yet, despite America's imperfect history, it is inarguably the closest thing the human race has ever produced to a Utopia. We have produced unparalleled levels of prosperity, technological advancement, scientific advancement, medical advancement, employment opportunities, entrepreneurial opportunities, charitable giving, and on and on and on. The failures of America have largely occurred when we have lost sight of those ideals and concepts that made us great—particularly our belief in the sovereignty of the individual.

John Winthrop, first governor of the Massachusetts Bay Colony, foresaw the coming greatness of America when he referred to the original American colonies as "the City on the Hill." Ronald Reagan picked up Winthrop's refrain and often referred to "the Shining City on the Hill" throughout his political career. The "Hill" described by both Winthrop and Reagan is the foundation of God and His principles.

In recent years, that foundation has begun to crumble due to neglect. Tragically, this paradise called America is on the road to becoming Paradise Lost.

In God We Trust?

Just twenty-two words: "Almighty God, we acknowledge our dependence upon Thee, and we beg Thy blessings upon us, our parents, our teachers, and our country." Those twenty-two words were formulated by an interfaith council composed of ministers, priests, and rabbis. Their purpose was to enable students of the state of New York to have a brief moment of reflection on God at the start of their day. But those few words sparked a battle that went all the way to the United States Supreme Court.

The case was *Engel v. Vitale*, 1962. In that case a parent named Steven Engel brought suit against the local board of education, alleging that this twenty-two-word prayer violated his child's First Amendment rights. These words, Engel argued, constituted "the establishment of religion" by the New York State Board of Regents.

Even though the Supreme Court recognized that this brief prayer was completely neutral, nonsectarian, and voluntary, the justices—in an opinion written by Justice Hugo Black—ruled this prayer unconstitutional. Since the

1962 decision, it has been virtually impossible for *any* prayers to be offered at *any* time in public schools.

Poll after poll tells us that between 75 and 80 percent of all Americans would like to see common prayer in their schools. Even the students themselves want the freedom to pray. In June 1991—after the California State Supreme Court ruled that there could no longer be prayers or benedictions at public school graduations—high school students in Yucca Valley (near Palm Springs) came up with an idea for bringing God back into their commencement exercises. The valedictorian walked up to the podium to give his speech—but the first sound from his mouth was not, "Parents, faculty, and fellow students," but, "Ahhhhhh-Choooooo!" A humongous *sneeze*! The entire student body rose up as one and shouted back, "God bless you!"

Students *want* God in their schools! But our government institutions have banned Him from the campus.

What has happened since the Supreme Court outlawed God? Well, since that 1962 decision, there has been a relentless, full-scale retreat from anything in public life that acknowledges God. We are not only taking God out of the classroom, but out of the public square, out of the marketplace, and out of the public discourse. Here are just a few examples out of a torrent of attacks on religious freedom which flow from the bitter spring of *Engel v. Vitale*:

- In a Colorado case, a public schoolteacher was forbidden to leave his Bible sitting on his desk where students might see it, even though he only read it during his free time.
- In Virginia, a ten-year-old girl who brought her Bible to school with her to read on the bus was told by the principal to leave her Bible at home.
- A fourth-grader in Massachusetts was told she could not draw Christian crosses in her art project.

- A Kentucky law authorized posters featuring the Ten Commandments to be hung in public school classrooms. The posters would be printed at private, not public, expense. The purpose of the posters was not to promote religion, but to acquaint students with the moral pillars of the legal code of their culture. The U.S. Supreme Court, however, didn't feel the students had a right to know about the Ten Commandments and struck down the Kentucky law in 1980. But the supreme irony of this tragic story is that, even as the decision was being read in the courtroom of the U.S. Supreme Court, there on the courtroom wall were inscribed—you guessed it!—those very same Ten Commandments!
- In 1989, seventeen-year-old Scott McDaniel, an Atlanta high school student, handed a note to a friend between classes. The assistant principal demanded the note, which was immediately turned over. It was an invitation for Scott's friend to attend an off-campus meeting of the Fellowship of Christian Athletes. The assistant principal threatened Matt with suspension for "possession of Christian materials"!

Understand, the original purpose of the First Amendment was to protect religious expression. Today, however, we are increasingly seeing the First Amendment used as an instrument of *oppression* against religion! This is the very tyranny that the early colonists came here to escape!

We need to understand how our religious liberty was intended to function. Unfortunately, there is a great deal of revisionist history being taught to our young people. The religious foundations of our country are being denigrated. The character and reputations of our founding fathers are being slandered. Children are taught that Thanksgiving was the day Pilgrims came to thank the Indians—not God!—for corn. In many schools, the word

Thanksgiving is no longer used, because it invites the question, "*Who* are we thanking?" So we call it "Fall Festival." And we call Christmas "Winter Break." And we call Easter "Spring Break." It is all part of a deliberate and diabolical effort to remove God and godly principles from the public square.

Let me ask you a question: Where are the following statements found?

(1) "Congress shall make no law respecting an establishment of religion, or prohibiting the free exercise thereof."

(2) "In order to ensure to citizens freedom of conscience, the church is separated from the state, and the school from the church. Freedom of religious worship is recognized for all citizens."

When asked this question, many people see the phrase in statement 2 which reads "the church is separated from the state," and conclude that this is the famous "separation of church and state" principle they have always heard about. "Statement 2," they say, "is from the Constitution."

Statement 1 is the opening clause of the First Amendment of the Constitution. Where does Statement 2 come from? From the Constitution of the now-defunct Soviet Union—a country that was specifically founded on atheist principles! Yet if you compare the direction our society is moving, and the direction the courts are moving, you would have to conclude that the U.S. Supreme Court is basing its decisions on the Constitution of the old USSR! Nowhere in the U.S. Constitution can you find the phrase "separation of church and state"! It's not in there! Instead, you find a very clear protection of the *free exercise* of religion. This simple truth must be rediscovered and reimplemented in American life—or we are doomed.

Without God and godly principles, we have nothing to base our concept of morality on. If there is no agreed-upon standard of morality, then who's to say what's right and what's wrong? The result is the rise of pornography, the overt display of homosexuality, increasing rates of rape, incest, and sexually transmitted disease, and even the surfacing of groups which openly advocate the legalization of pedophilia (sex with children).

And let's face it: It gets right down to our pocketbooks, and to the future of our children. This country is running up trillions of dollars of debt that it will never be able to repay. In fact, within a few years, it will take every penny of tax revenue we now take in just to pay the *interest* on the debt! How did we get into this mess? Not because there's a problem with our economy. It's because of the runaway selfishness of various groups who demand their take from the public trough (from welfare to farm subsidies to corporate giveaway programs), coupled with the cowardice of politicians who put their own re-election ahead of the fate of the country. Our economic woes are really a moral problem. This is a "sin tax" we are paying.

A Godly Secular Nation

The respect for human sovereignty and decisionability has given us our wonderful American freedom and our amazing American prosperity. It has given every person in this country, from the poorest to the richest, complete access to the American dream and the pursuit of happiness.

It is the *misuse* of our human sovereignty that has given us a crime epidemic, an AIDS epidemic, a child-abuse epidemic, and an abortion epidemic. The misuse of our decisionability bleeds our economy, bloats the welfare state, expands the police state, and feeds a hungry military-industrial complex.

If the people of the world would accept the responsibility of their own sovereignty, then choose to submit their own will to God's will, much—perhaps most!—of the hunger and suffering in this world could be eliminated. Despite everything you've heard about famines in Africa, Asia, or the Indian subcontinent, there is enough food to feed all the people in the world—more than enough! When people go hungry somewhere in the world, it is rarely because of bad climate or natural disaster. Almost invariably it is because of bad choices, inflicted on a population by bad leaders. Their hunger for power and domination leaves the common people hungry for rice and beans. If we would repent and beat our swords into plowshares, if the poor nations of the world would buy tractors instead of tanks, there would be no starvation.

If you disagree, then just consider the nation of Iraq. Some Bible scholars believe that the Garden of Eden was once located there. That country has some of the richest oil reserves in the world, plus huge amounts of arable land for food production. If it weren't for the greed and power-mad ambitions of Saddam Hussein, and his lust to conquer neighboring Kuwait, Iraq would be a wealthy nation today. If all the money and man-hours spent in wars against Iran, Kuwait, and the U.S.-led Desert Storm coalition had been spent instead in improving the lives of the Iraqi people, that country could be a veritable Garden of Eden again!

Why don't these nations see the wisdom of voluntarily, volitionally beating their swords into plowshares? Because the only lens through which this wisdom can be seen is the Gospel of Jesus Christ. Without the Gospel, they can only keep on doing what they've always been doing: warring, power-grabbing, poisoning not only their neighbors' land but their own. The Gospel has an enormous lifting and elevating power that other religions don't offer.

The wise principles of the Bible were never embedded in the founding documents of Iraq or Ethiopia or Somalia. The warlords of those nations do not recognize the sovereignty of their people. They declare themselves to be the sovereign masters of their own countries—and their people pay the price.

America is great because America is the land that states in the very first line of its Constitution, in letters far larger than any other words on the page, "We the People"! What an exalted, thrilling, elevating concept: We the People! We the sovereign People of the United States! We the free People, entrusted by God and our founding fathers with the right to choose our own destiny! We the People, made in the likeness and image of God! Once we have begun to grasp the enormity and power that is ours as sovereign individuals, living in a society of sovereigns, there is no telling how far and how high we can go!

Rhonda Grimes was once a welfare mother and a cocaine addict. She came from a welfare-dependent family and had never known any other way to live. She couldn't read, couldn't write, and had no job skills. Still, she had managed to kick her coke habit and was hoping that someday she would get her life together.

One day, Rhonda was in the welfare office, filling out some forms. The eligibility worker told her she would have to lie on her paperwork in order to stay on welfare. Rhonda was horrified. "I wasn't going to lie," she later recalled. "I spent most of my life in this system. My entire family is in the system, but I found it teaches you to lie and cheat just to stay on."

She realized that by living her life as a ward of the state, she was enslaved by the system. "Welfare is bondage," she concluded. "It's no different from the bondage of drug addiction." She became so angry with the system that enslaved her and tried to steal her integrity that she quit accepting the government checks. To support her family, she started doing housecleaning.

Just two months into her new job as a self-employed housecleaner, Rhonda was bringing home $2,000 a month in earnings. She put together a business plan, and is now adding employees and forming a housecleaning business. She is also working with a group of investors to open a drug rehab center for women—a dream of hers growing out of her own struggle with cocaine. She wants to dispense compassion to needy people without handouts or government bureaucracy.

"I didn't want these people controlling me for the rest of my life. I didn't want to stay locked in. I'm now free." Rhonda Grimes doesn't need the government to give her another program to make her successful. She is succeeding on her own terms, making her own choices, making her own way in life. Rhonda Grimes is *free* because she has discovered the key which unlocks all of life: her own God-given sovereignty.

In the next chapter, we will see how our God-given sovereignty affects one of the most important human relationships which God has designed for us to experience: the marriage relationship.

7

THE UNION OF TWO SOVEREIGNS

Marriage is a deep, significant, and spiritual act. Marriage is nothing less than the union of two sovereign individuals. If you don't understand that, then when you get married, you will not be able to enjoy what marriage *is*. You won't even enjoy living with one another if you don't understand this principle: *You don't have to if you don't want to.* You don't have to be married.

In fact, Scripture teaches that for certain individuals in certain situations, being single is preferable to being married. In 1 Corinthians chapter 7, we discover what marriage is supposed to be like, according to God's plan. But this passage also tells us that we don't have to be married —and why:

> He who is unmarried cares for the things of the Lord—
> how he may please the Lord. But he who is married cares
> about the things of the world—how he may please his wife
> (1 Cor. 7:32, 33).

God designed you to be a "sovereign you." You reach young adulthood with 360 degrees of freedom radiating in all directions. You don't have to account to anybody, nor do you have to take anybody else into account. You can set goals, make plans, and take risks—and you don't have to worry about how those goals, plans, and risks will affect anyone else. When you are single, you are free to do whatever you want to do—including (if you so choose) devoting yourself fully to serving the Lord.

But when you marry, that changes. Your freedom is conditional, you now have to plan for two, and you have to consider how your actions and risk-taking might affect your partner in life. This does not mean that being single is better than being married. It simply means that the two states are different. The single state offers some advantages for the person who wants to be free to serve God in a singleminded way.

It's okay to remain single. If you have any serious second thoughts or mental reservations, *don't do it.* It is better to say, "Hey! Chill! Time out!" in the middle of the ceremony and scandalize six hundred guests than to commit the balance of your life to a mistake.

Negotiating Your Surrender

The report of Ananias and Sapphira in Acts 5 is not a teaching about marriage, but it has a lot of bearing on the kind of commitment two people make when they say, "I do." In this record, Ananias and his wife, Sapphira, sell a piece of land and bring part of the proceeds to the apostles as a gift to the Lord. They also hold back part of the proceeds. Nothing wrong with that.

But there is one thing Ananias and Sapphira do that is terribly wrong: They lie. They claim to have sold land and given the entire proceeds to God. As a result of their deception—and as an example to the church—both of them are supernaturally struck dead, first Ananias and then Sapphira.

Before judgment falls on Ananias, the apostle Peter says to him, "While it remained, was it not your own? And after it was sold, was it not in your own control? Why have you conceived this thing in your heart? You have not lied to men but to God" (Acts 5:4). In other words, "Ananias, the land was yours, the money was yours, and you could do anything you wanted to with it. You don't have to give it to God if you don't want to. It's your sovereign choice. You could have given all, given half, given 10 percent, or kept it. But you lied about your choice—and that was your undoing."

Now, what does this story have to do with marriage? Your life is like that piece of land or the money that Ananias and Sapphira got for the land. You can do whatever you want with it. You want to stay single? You want to get married? That's up to you! You can if you want to. You don't have to if you don't want to. Your life is yours—until you marry. Once you marry, you make a voluntary choice to surrender a measure of your sovereignty to your spouse.

What is the purpose of the courtship phase of a relationship? It is the period when you and the person you are attracted to begin negotiating the surrender of a measure of your sovereignty! By the time you reach the altar and say, "I do," you should already have reached a point in your mind where you fully understand and agree to the fact that marriage entails surrender.

Unfortunately, many of us in the pastoral ministry fail to make this clear in premarital counseling, so many couples come to the marriage altar not fully understanding what they are doing. Once the couple has been pronounced "man and wife," the lives of these two people have been dramatically altered. They are no longer free to consider only their own individual desires; they have each handed over to the other—willingly and deliberately—a measure of their God-given sovereignty.

———

The Two Sovereigns Become One

God said to Moses, "I AM WHO I AM" (Ex. 3:14). When two people come together at the marriage altar, each of them is a sovereign "I am," made in the image of the great and omnipotent "I AM." As they commit themselves to a lifetime together before the assembled witnesses of their union, they each bring their self-awareness, self-will, and sovereignty. These two sovereign beings, these two "I ams," are asked to make a decision of their own free will.

At any point in this process, either one of these two sovereign individuals can say, "No, I can't promise that." The man can say, "You mean I have to love only this one woman for the rest of my life? No, I'm sorry, I just can't do that. I'm not ready for that. Let's call this thing off." And the woman can say, "You mean I have to respect and obey this man? No way! Stop the music. Keep your ring. I'm outta here."

And that's the end of it!

But if they both choose to say, "Yes, I do, I will," to all the questions they are asked at the altar, if they are pronounced husband and wife in the presence of all these witnesses, then they are no longer two separate entities. They are one.

Now, we do not become slaves at the wedding. Though we agree to surrender a measure of our sovereignty, we don't become less than what we were. We are actually expanded and magnified. Just as our personhood is increased when we surrender to Christ, so the surrender of our sovereignty in marriage makes us more than we were before. As Jesus said, "Give, and it will be given to you" (Luke 6:38).

The Ideal Meets the Real

Charles Laughton, the great English actor who portrayed Captain Bligh in *Mutiny on the Bounty* (1935), was married to actress Elsa Lanchester. An interviewer once asked him, "If you were widowed or divorced, would you ever consider marrying again?"

"No!" Laughton responded flatly, surprising the interviewer with his bluntness.

"Why is that?"

"Because," said Laughton, "during courtship, a man reveals only his better side. After marriage, however, his real self begins to come out—and it's too late for a wife to do anything about it." He paused a moment, then added, "I wouldn't put another woman through that again."

Laughton was describing a process universal to all marriages: Two unique, sovereign individuals combine to form one sovereign union. It all starts with romance and ideal images of married bliss. But soon after the wedding, the problems set in. Often, the husband has his agenda, the wife has hers: "We have to do it this way, my parents always did it that way." Suddenly Mr. Right is a total slob who always leaves the toilet seat up. Suddenly Miss Right is a gripy old lady who hangs her stockings in the shower and squeezes the toothpaste from the middle. That little laugh that used to send thrills up his spine now sounds kind of silly. And his penchant for witty remarks and humor now seems embarrassingly lame.

That's the point when disillusionment sets in. Suddenly one or both parties is feeling increasingly unhappy and frustrated in the relationship. Why? Because the ideal has collided with the real.

In the beginning, the ideal existed in the mind of God. Then He spoke the ideal into existence, and the ideal became real. God said, "Let there be light" (Gen. 1:3), and there was light, and it was good. There was no gap between the ideal and the real. Then sin came into the world, and a huge gulf opened up between the ideal and the real. In life, the space between the ideal and the real is what we call *disappointment*. We're disappointed when the ideal and the real don't match up.

So "some enchanted evening," when a man and woman see each other "across a crowded room," each says, "This is my dream, this is my ideal." The fair maiden and the knight in shining armor come together to ride off into the sunset and live happily ever after—but soon their steed begins to falter and stumble beneath the weight of one disappointment after another. Their storybook castle becomes a three-bedroom, suburban dungeon of despair.

As the ideal evaporates and reality sets in, angry words, misunderstandings, and hurts accumulate and are stored up. I call these grievances "insults to one's sovereignty." On some level, we all know that we have a right to have our God-given sovereignty respected by other people, and especially by our mate. When we feel our sovereignty has been insulted, we think—and justifiably so!—*I don't have to put up with this! I'm just as much a sovereign as you are! My rights and my feelings are just as important as yours are! My free will is just as important as yours!*

One common complaint in husband-wife relationships —particularly in Christian marriages—comes from the wife: "He doesn't respect my feelings and my wishes. He says, 'I'm the head of the household. What I say, goes.'" Even in this era of militant feminism and equal rights for women, this issue is a common tension in marriages. Many men continue to treat their wives as inferior—and men who do this are violating the sovereignty of their wives, and they are violating God's intentions.

When God created Adam and Eve, He made them equal co-sovereigns. He didn't make Eve out of Adam's neck so that she could be that which turns his head. He didn't make Eve out of Adam's back so she could be his spine. He didn't make Eve out of his foot so he could walk on her. He created her out of Adam's side to be beside him. A man was never intended by God to lord it over his wife. She is a partner, a mate, an equal—not a slave or a subject.

Now, this is crucial: The fact that men and women were created *equal* does not mean that they were made the *same*. Men and women are very different. Obviously, they are physically different. But they also think differently, feel differently, and communicate differently, as recent books have documented (see *You Just Don't Understand* by Deborah Tannen, and *Men Are from Mars, Women Are from Venus* by John Gray). Researchers have even found that there are anatomical differences between men and women that explain their psychological and emotional differences.

The source of a great deal of disillusionment in marriage relationships is that each partner has his or her ideal—and that ideal soon collides with the real. The husband finds out that this woman who used to be his sweet and charming dream date is now a *wife*, just like every other wife. Suddenly, he realizes he's lost the sovereignty he took for granted when he was single.

And the wife finds out this man who was so sweet and considerate of her needs and feelings while they were dating has somehow become a *husband* like every other husband. This makes her feel that she's lost the sovereignty and freedom she took for granted when she was single.

If these two people are not careful, they will unwittingly allow grievances, grudges, and insults to pile until they are no longer able to relate to each other. To avert potential disaster, they should:

1. Recognize that each partner in the marriage is a sovereign, with rights and feelings that must be respected.

You may not agree with each other on every issue, but you can respect the other's feelings on any issue.

2. Communicate with each other as one king relates to another. Respect the rights and free will of each other. Complete respect is much more important than complete agreement in holding a relationship together.

3. Take personal responsibility for sovereign choices and actions rather than assigning blame.

In 1840, three years after her coronation, England's Queen Victoria married Prince Albert. A few weeks after their wedding, the Queen and the Prince had a royal spat that ended with shouting, foot-stamping, and door-slamming. Prince Albert harrumphed up to his private quarters and locked the door. Queen Victoria grumped around for a few minutes, then stormed on up the stairs to finish the argument. She arrived at the door of her husband's quarters, tried the knob, and found the door locked. Now she was really in a lather! So she hammered furiously on the door. "Let me in!" she demanded.

"Who's there?" asked the Prince from the other side of the door.

"You know perfectly well who it is," shouted Victoria. "It is the Queen of England, and she demands to be admitted!"

The Queen's demand was met with silence. So she pounded on the door again.

"Who's there?" the Prince asked again.

"The Queen of England," Victoria reiterated, "and she *still* demands to be admitted!"

More silence. The door remained shut and locked. Again the Queen pounded on the door.

This time, only silence.

The Queen raised her fist to pound on the door again—then she paused. After a few moments' reflection, she tapped lightly on the door, a gentle, almost hesitant little knock.

"Who's there?" asked the Prince.

"Albert, dear," said the Queen, "it is your wife."

Within seconds, Prince Albert opened the door. The argument was over. Even if one partner in a marriage is the Queen of England, the key to opening the door of communication is to respect the other partner's God-given sovereignty.

————

At the Altar

The wedding ceremony is a beautiful portrayal of deep spiritual truths, conveyed through powerful, meaningful symbols. Consider, for a moment, the symbols of the wedding ceremony and what they represent: The groom stands at the altar, accompanied by his best man and the minister. These three men symbolize the Holy Trinity: The minister represents the Father, the groom represents the Son, the best man represents the Holy Spirit. These three are waiting for something. What are they waiting for? An incredible vision of loveliness: the bride.

Soon the music swells, and all eyes turn to the rear of the sanctuary, and there, approaching down the center aisle, is the bride. She sweeps up the altar—and what is she? She is a sovereign being possessing beauty, skills, talent, passions, charm, fire, and intellect. She is an incredibly complex creature; the groom will spend the rest of his life getting to know her, and even at the end of his life there will be layers of mystery and intrigue about her that he has yet to unravel. She is radiant in clouds of white lace and gauzy veils. There is an aura, a halo of wonder all about her. She is one of the great mysteries of the universe. She is Woman.

Here they stand, the bride and the groom. Do these two people—who are so young and just beginning to enter the world as adults—really understand what they are doing? The minister says a few words to reinforce both the joy and the seriousness of what they are about to do.

Then the minister addresses the man and says, "Do you take this woman?" This is a solemn question, directed to a sovereign man. He is being called upon to acknowledge his free will and decisionability. He does not have to say yes. He is perfectly free, in the sight of God and all these witnesses, to say, "No, I've changed my mind. I do not take her." And that's the end of it. She goes back to her father, to her home, and he has no further responsibility for her.

And what if this sovereign man chooses to say yes? Is he willing to faithfully devote himself only to this one woman and, forsaking all others, cling only to her? If, after considering these questions in their full weight and import, he can say, "I do," then a sovereign choice has been made.

But that doesn't end the matter. There is another individual at this altar. She is not a piece of property. She is volitional and sovereign in her own right. So the minister turns to the woman and asks, "Do you take this man?"

Another solemn question, calling this woman to be fully aware of her own free will and decisionability. She is perfectly free, in the sight of all these witnesses, to say, "No, I will not." If she says, "No," that is the end of it. The people in the pews may gasp. Old Aunt Martha may faint, and the flower girl may giggle. But this woman has a God-given right to close the matter right there at the altar.

In most cases, however, she says, "I do." Now, both the man and the woman have made their covenant, said their vows, and sealed their solemn contract in the sight of God and their friends and family. The minister pronounces them married. These two sovereign individuals now make up one sovereign unit. They must now spend the rest of their lives working out that choice. They can build something beautiful and enduring on the foundation of that choice—or they can make it a hell on earth. It is their sovereign choice.

The Covenant

Many people marry at an age when they are just coming to grips with their newfound liberty. They are bouncing off the walls with excitement over the fact that they are out on their own, making their own way, no longer answerable to Daddy and Momma. Finally they have the liberty to do whatever they want to—but they get out on the streets and into the workplace, and they discover that the responsibility for their existence falls squarely on their own shoulders. They are shocked to discover that there aren't many people out there who really care about them.

But then they find that one person who "really cares," they fall in love and get married. "It's us against the world," they think, and everything is wonderful—for a while.

Soon, however, a realization sets in: The wonderful liberty they achieved upon leaving their parents' home has now been traded in for something called "marriage." They may feel trapped. They may even want to get their liberty back. If a fight erupts or if they feel their personhood is challenged, they may want to "Drop off the key, Lee. Hit the road, Jack." This is a major reason why so many marriages fall apart. Couples are often not prepared to shoulder the responsibility they have taken on. They have never adequately considered the solemnity of the choice they have made. In an age of casual relationships and "significant others," an age in which society exerts no pressure on couples to honor their commitments, it becomes easy for one or both parties to simply back out.

What few couples realize is that a marriage vow is not a conditional promise. Most other contracts we make in our everyday life—insurance policies, leases, mortgages, employment contracts, and the like—are conditional promises: "If you do this, I will do that." A marriage contract is infinitely more solemn. It is the most solemn agreement two people can make.

Why?

Because it is a *blood covenant.*

In the Bible, there is no covenant more sacred and inviolate than the blood covenant. When God wanted to make His covenant with Abram, He made a blood covenant, involving the death of innocent animals. This blood covenant is the basis for Abraham's remarkable faith. In Genesis 21, when God told Abraham to take his only son Isaac up on the mountain and sacrifice him, Abraham was able to trust God and instantly obey because God had made a blood covenant with Abraham to give him many descendants—and no one can break a blood covenant, least of all God!

At the Passover meal, just before going to the cross, Jesus said to His disciples, "This is My blood of the new covenant, which is shed for many for the remission of sins" (Matt. 26:28). He was underscoring the seriousness and solemnity of the new covenant God was making with mankind by sending His Son to the cross. It would be the most sacred covenant of all: a blood covenant.

Throughout Scripture, God promises, "I will never leave you nor forsake you." How do we know we can trust God's assurance that He will never leave us nor forsake us? Because God has sealed this promise with a blood covenant. He is bound by His honor. God has given us His word and His blood covenant. It is impossible for God to lie.

God takes His word, His promises, and His honor seriously! What of our own word, our promises, our honor? Once we have entered into this blood covenant, we have committed ourselves to this covenant for all time. The blood covenant of marriage is the most sacred and inviolate covenant we ever make.

"Hold it right there, Ben! Why are you calling marriage a 'blood covenant'? I've been to a lot of weddings and I've never seen any blood shed. Well, maybe at the reception . . ."

The blood covenant is something which takes place between the man and the bride *after* the wedding ceremony, on the wedding night. The biblical ideal is for these two people to retire to the marriage chamber, bringing their virginity to each other as a sacred, once-in-a-lifetime gift. There, before God and in each other's presence, they seal this holy, spiritual, physical, emotional, legal union through the mutual giving of themselves in sexual intercourse. They unite in a holy act of mutual surrender. It is an act that was once described by a word we hardly hear anymore: They *consummate* their marriage.

What is this act of consummation? It centers around the fact that a virgin woman has a thin, totally useless membrane called the hymen, which is stretched across the entrance to her vagina. When the man penetrates the woman's vagina, he ruptures the hymen. The hymen bleeds and that blood covers his parts. The virginal blood that is shed there upon the marriage bed represents the blood covenant of the marriage. For further reading, see *Communication, Sex, Money* by Edwin Louis Cole (Honor Books, Tulsa, OK, 1987).

"Oh, come off it, Ben! That's out of left field!" Oh? Deuteronomy 22, which contains some of the laws of Israel governing marriage and morality, describes a situation where a man marries a young lady, then after intercourse on their wedding night he decides he doesn't like what he finds, so he falsely and publicly accuses the poor innocent girl of not being a virgin. In effect, he accuses her of the serious crime of promiscuity. The Scriptures record that parents of the young woman would have already gone to the marriage chamber and gathered up "the evidence of the young woman's virginity." To answer the man's accusation against their daughter, they would now bring that evidence to the elders of the people.

Now, what is this evidence? It is the bedclothes and bed linens used by the couple on their wedding night. Those clothes and linens would be stained with blood—the evidence that the woman's hymen had broken during sexual intercourse, and that she was indeed a virgin. The parents would take these linens, fold them up, and keep them carefully in a safe place, so that if their son-in-law ever came back and said, "I find her not a virgin," then they can spread the evidence before the elders and say, "Here is the blood. This man has lied, and he has slandered the reputation of a virgin in Israel." In the New Testament, Jesus affirms this Old Testament law in Matthew 5:32 and 19:9.

Now the words, "till death do us part," take on a whole new meaning. Husbands and wives, the promise you made at the altar before God and all those witnesses was not just something you can undo if "it doesn't work out" or if "we're just incompatible." The blood covenant of marriage is one of the most sacred and inviolable contracts you could ever enter into. Malachi 2:16 says, "God . . . hates divorce." And Jesus says, "Therefore what God has joined together, let not man separate" (Matt. 19.6). God loves people, and broken marriage covenants hurt the people He loves, bringing pain to husbands, wives, families, and especially children. So God hates divorce.

Now, this doesn't mean that there is no recovery from divorce. It is not the unforgiveable sin. God knows we are imperfect people who sin and fail and violate our promises. There is grace and forgiveness. But we dare not take the blood covenant of marriage lightly. This solemn covenant was instituted by God for our protection and benefit, and we violate it at our own peril. We need to understand the consequence of breaking a blood covenant—an act which God calls *treachery*. In Malachi 2:14, God explains to Israel why its prayers go unheard:

> Because the LORD has been witness
> Between you and the wife of your youth,
> With whom you have dealt treacherously;
> Yet she is your companion
> And your wife by covenant.

When you make a blood covenant, you keep it. When you marry, you stay with your spouse "till death you do part." No one forced you into this covenant. Even at the altar, you could have said "No." You went into it with your eyes wide open, freely and volitionally, exercising your sovereign decisionability.

Just before the great scriptural treatise on marriage in 1 Corinthians 7, there is a profound section dealing with interpersonal relationships. Many Christians would never think of applying the opening verses of chapter 6 to marriage, but I believe they are intensely relevant:

> Dare any of you, having a matter against another, go to law
> before the unrighteous, and not before the saints? Do you
> not know that the saints will judge the world? And if the
> world will be judged by you, are you unworthy to judge
> the smallest matters? Do you not know that we shall judge
> angels? How much more, things that pertain to this life?"
> (1 Cor. 6:1–3).

When the Bible talks about taking a matter to the courts, doesn't that apply to divorce court as well? And doesn't it also apply to other sources of secular "wisdom" that people rely on for insight into marital problems— secular counselors, articles in secular magazines, and talk shows like "Oprah" and "Sally" and "Geraldo"? As Psalm

1:1 reminds us, "Blessed is the man [or woman!]/Who walks not in the counsel of the ungodly"! We are going to judge the world! We are going to judge the angels! So we should not be ordering our marriages or planning for divorce according to the counsel of the ungodly oracles of our society. If we can't order our own lives and our own households, how will we reign with Jesus in the world to come?

Another important aspect of the blood covenant of marriage is that it underscores the importance of keeping oneself sexually pure before marriage. Looking at the wedding night from the perspective of God's ideal, when a nonvirgin couple marries and retires to the bedchamber, it is impossible for the blood covenant to take place. There is no blood shed on the wedding night. Am I saying nonvirgins should not get married? Of course not. I'm saying they have missed out on a key element of God's plan for marriage by engaging in sexual intercourse outside of God's intended timing and boundaries. God is gracious, and He helps us to overcome our sins and mistakes. But we are so much better off if we can avoid those sins and mistakes in the first place.

Happily, there are indications that virginity and sexual abstinence before marriage are making a comeback. Amid horrible reports of rising incidents of teenage AIDS and other sexually transmitted diseases, amid all the talk of distributing condoms in high schools, junior highs, and even grammar schools, there is a surge of interest among teenagers in what is called "virgin cool." That is, it's actually becoming "cool" to remain a virgin! An organization called "True Love Waits" has been founded to raise teenage awareness and encourage teens to make a commitment to remain pure until marriage. Hundreds of thousands of teens have made the True Love Waits commitment to sexual purity before marriage.

NBA All-Star A. C. Green has been bringing basketball

fans to their feet for over ten years, first with the L.A. Lakers and now with the Phoenix Suns. He is also a dedicated Christian and founder of A. C. Green Programs for Youth and Athletes for Abstinence. In his book *Victory*, he writes,

> I am sick of people being sold a false bill of goods. It's great to let people know their options, but the options given today are faulty. We need a higher standard by which to govern our sexuality. Young people are told when they're old enough to smoke, drink, drive, vote, go to school, and fight in the military, but we don't tell them when they can have sex.
>
> Out of deep concern, during my sixth year in the NBA, I formed Athletes for Abstinence to teach that the only 100-percent sure way to avoid STDs, unwanted pregnancies, and a lot of the consequences of ending a sexual relationship is sexual abstinence. We teach that sex in itself is not wrong and was actually created by God, but that sex *outside of marriage* is not worth the risks. Just because everyone else is doing it doesn't mean that it's right. And besides, everyone *isn't* doing it. They're just saying they are, the way I did as a kid.
>
> Even if you've been sexually active, it's never too late to say no. You can't go back, but you can go forward. . . . If you can control yourself sexually, you can control yourself, period.
>
> A. C. Green, *Victory* (Lake Mary, FL: Creation House, 1994) pp. 130–31.

When we join sexually with another person, we become one with that person. We enter into a covenant with that person. That's why we should join with no other person but our spouse; why husbands and wives should never have sex outside of marriage; why young people should not engage in premarital sex; why a man should never have sex with a prostitute.

Sex is God's idea. His intention was to fuse two sovereign individuals into a single holy entity. Sex was never meant to be just another form of recreation like skiing or shooting baskets or going to the movies. Sex is an act that initiates and celebrates a solemn covenant. It is an act in which two become one in the eyes of God.

Ray had lived a wild life before he married Lisa. But when Ray met Lisa, he knew she was something very special, and he wanted to spend his life with her. At one point in their courtship, she asked him point-blank if he had ever been sexually involved with anyone else—and Ray lied. "No," he said. "I've kept myself pure."

About two years after they were married, Lisa developed some suspicious health problems. She went to the doctor and was shocked when she was diagnosed as having a sexually transmitted disease. "That's impossible!" she said. "There must be some mistake!"

"No mistake," said the doctor. "The chances of getting this disease in any other way are virtually zero."

So Lisa went home and confronted Ray with the medical report. At first, he tried to deny that he had given her this disease—then he admitted it. "Okay, you're right," he confessed. "I lied before when I said I had kept myself pure before marriage. I was involved with a woman before I met you."

"Just one woman?"

"Actually, several women."

"How many is 'several'?"

"Half a dozen. Maybe a dozen."

"A dozen?"

"Plus a few one-night stands. I got this disease from one of them and—well, I guess I gave it to you. I'm sorry."

"You're sorry." The look of hurt on Lisa's face made Ray cringe.

"Honest, Lisa, that's all in the past. It happened before I ever met you. I swear I've been faithful."

"You swear, do you? Before we were married, you swore you'd never been with another woman. You were lying then, weren't you? Or were you? Maybe you were telling the truth then, but you're lying now. Maybe you've been running around on me since we were married. Or maybe you've *always* been lying and running around."

"Believe me! I'm telling you the absolute truth!"

"Why should I believe you? Why should I have anything to do with you? Ray, I'm risking my life anytime I go to bed with you! For all I know, you could have already given me AIDS, and I wouldn't know it for years!"

"Flee sexual immorality," the Word tells us. "Every sin that a man does is outside the body, but he who commits sexual immorality sins against his own body" (1 Cor. 6:18). And, by extension, sexual immorality is a sin against one's spouse, because the two sovereigns have become one sovereign union. The person who abuses God's gift of sex violates his own body, the body of his spouse, the body of his sexual partner, and the blood covenant of marriage.

The key to a healthy, satisfying marriage lies in recognizing and accepting the fact that you didn't have to get married. It was a choice you entered into of your own sovereign free will. Now that you have made that choice, now that you have entered into that solemn blood covenant with your spouse, in the eyes of God, what are you going to do?

If you choose to break that covenant—through adultery, divorce, spouse abuse, or whatever—then I guarantee you this: You will experience a hurt that you can't even imagine until you go through it. And that hurt will radiate out to others—to the very people you are charged with protecting and loving and encouraging. In your sovereign free will, you have the power to bring down all that pain and harm upon yourself and upon your family.

But if you choose to bind yourself and your honor to

the blood covenant you have made, then there is every possibility that you will experience the most satisfying, stimulating, joy-filled adventure imaginable: the lifelong journey of two sovereign human beings, joined at the heart, welded at the soul, fused at the spirit. And in all of life, there is nothing more beautiful than that.

8

THE MYSTERY AND THE MEANING

A famous ballerina was once asked if she was in favor of the feminist movement. "Not if it means I have to carry Rudolf Nureyev around!" she exclaimed. "I want *him* to carry *me!*"

In ballet and in marriage, there are roles for women and roles for men. If, out of some misplaced, misguided idea of "equality," we try to confuse those roles, all kinds of problems ensue. In the previous chapter, I made two statements which many people might view as inconsistent. I said that (1) men and women were created equal and co-sovereign; and (2) husbands have a leadership and guardianship role in the marriage. You might be thinking, "Whoa! Hold it right there, Ben! If the woman is equal to the man, how can you say that man has a leadership and guardianship role? Doesn't the word 'leadership' mean 'superior position'?"

Absolutely not! Men and women are equal, totally and unequivocally. A man is sovereign; so is a woman. But the fact that the sexes are *equal* does not mean the sexes are the *same*.

As I read the flow of God's Word regarding the husband-wife relationship, it is clear that the husband is the head of the union. "For the husband is head of the wife, as also Christ is head of the church; and He is the Savior of the body" (Eph. 5:23). The Bible compares the husband's role toward the wife with Christ's role toward the church —and the apostle Paul points specifically to two functions which Christ performs for the church: Christ is the Head (which denotes leadership) and the Savior (the guardian and protector) of the church.

A husband, then, is intended and designed by God to exercise dominion, leadership, and guardianship for his home, his wife, and his children. God created him to provide for, defend, and love his wife and family, to carve out a place for his family in this great wilderness called life. That is not his status. That is his *role*. That is his *function*. He is not greater than his wife.

Marriage is not a king-subject or master-slave relationship. The husband is not the master of the wife; she is a co-sovereign and he serves her in his leadership capacity. The problem comes when we confuse roles with status, dominion with domination, and leadership with dictatorship.

Each sovereign partner in the marriage has a role to play. This doesn't mean that each role has to be a straitjacket, that the husband has to leave the house briefcase in hand at 7:37 every morning and return every evening at 5:23, and that his wife must spend the intervening time behind a vacuum cleaner or an ironing board. As sovereign, free moral agents, we have many options in life.

At the same time, we should understand that the *responsible* options that are open to married people are different than those for single people. The sovereign decisions a single man or woman makes affect no one else. If you want to sail around the world on a tramp steamer, and you have no obligations toward anyone else, then why not? If you want to be an actor, run for president, sell aluminum siding, join the French foreign legion, become an astronaut, or flip burgers under the Golden Arches, that's up to you.

But when you say, "I choose to be his wife," or, "I choose to be her husband," then you have really said, in effect, "I have used my mind to sift through all the various options that the full scope of life presents to me, and I know what I want. I want to be married for the rest of my life to this other sovereign individual." You are not restricted in your choices because you are black or white. You are not restricted because you are male, female, fat, thin, tall, or short. God has placed no restrictions on us. He has said, "All things are possible to him who believes" (Mark 9:23). You can get married if you want to; but, you don't have to if you don't want to.

You can compare the journey of your life to any other journey. First, you decide you want to take a trip. But where do you want to go? You could visit Mexico or Paris or the Caribbean or New York City or Sheboygan, Wisconsin. You think and consider all the options, and finally you decide: You want to go to Japan. Fine. Now what other options do you have? Well you could go as a missionary, a diplomat, a student, a businessperson, or a tourist. How will you get there? Well, you could fly (first-class or tourist?). Or you could take a ship. Or a hot-air balloon. Or you could buy a catamaran and sail the Pacific alone. Life is just like that: filled with endless options and opportunities.

After you have sorted through all your options, you are perfectly free to choose the option of marriage. When you choose that option, however, you are saying, "God, I surrender a measure of my sovereignty, including the right to choose other options as my primary option. I recognize the fact that by making myself the spouse of this person, I have set an additional goal of pleasing this other person, not just pleasing myself and striving for my own individual goals."

You may say at this point, "Now, wait just one moment! Are you saying, Ben, that if a woman becomes a wife, she can't be anything else, she can only be a wife and home-maker?" No, not at all! Just look at this description of the virtuous wife, excerpted from Proverbs 31. First, she dabbles in real estate and agriculture:

> She considers a field and buys it;
> From her profits she plants a vineyard (Prov. 31:16).

She runs her own business—and even burns the mid-night oil to get the job done:

> She perceives that her merchandise is good,
> And her lamp does not go out by night.
> She stretches out her hands to the distaff,
> And her hand holds the spindle (Prov. 31:18, 19).

She's involved in community work and charity:

> She extends her hand to the poor,
> Yes, she reaches out her hands to the needy (Prov. 31:20).

Is she a woman of the nineties or what? She even works out on the Nautilus machine at the health club! Listen to this:

> She girds herself with strength,
> And strengthens her arms (Prov. 31:17).

And she does all this while being a Class A wife and mother:

She watches over the ways of her household,
And does not eat the bread of idleness.
Her children rise up and call her blessed;
Her husband also, and he praises her:
"Many daughters have done well,
But you excel them all" (Prov. 31:27–29).

Some people scoff at this passage and say, "Well, that's a man talking!" But no, Proverbs 31 is the wisdom of a woman, the mother of King Lemuel. It is a passage written to give women a model of intelligent, competent, and accomplished womanhood. Such a woman, says Lemuel's mother, is worth more than rubies, and is a crown to her husband's head.

In God's plan, a wife is capable of doing and becoming virtually anything she wants—as long as she is faithful to her primary purpose, and to her blood covenant. She has made a covenant to be a wife, and that is now her primary purpose in life. She chose that. She made a sovereign decision. If there is a way she can be a wife and also be a vice president of marketing, that's just fine! She should sit down with her husband, and they should agree together on her role and his role. For as the Scriptures say, "Can two walk together, unless they are agreed?" (Amos 3:3.)

"Honey," she says, "I really feel called to be the vice president of marketing. I'm qualified, and I just got a great offer at a nice salary."

"Well," he says, "we have two children. What about them?"

"We can leave the children with a baby-sitter."

"Now, I'm not sure about this. You know, child development experts say these two little sovereign human beings we brought into the world get most of their imprinting during the first five years. Our kids are ages one and four. When they get to be school age, that's another matter, but right now I think they really need their mother to stay home with them."

"Well, why can't you stay home and mind the kids, and I can go to work?"

Now, that's a good question. But both Scripture and practical experience indicate that the husband-wife relationship doesn't usually work that way. Turning Dad into "Mr. Mom" and sending Mom off in the morning with a briefcase violates the way men and women are designed. This is not just a matter of social expectations or fragile male egos, as the feminists would have you believe. God gave to the man a role of dominion and guardianship, a role of providership and protectorship. It is built into men, and when you take that away from a man, you violate his design. When you disallow him from providing and leading his family, you often see a whole host of other problems arise: drug abuse, alcohol abuse, spouse abuse, and violence. Consider this:

A great deal of gang activity and street violence can actually be traced to the fact that young men have been displaced from their God-given roles as husband-providers, and have been replaced by a welfare check. They have been told by the government to stay away from the woman who is the mother of their children, or else the checks will stop coming. So what does this man do to create a sense of family, a sense of dominion, a sense of ego-mastery? He takes it to the streets. He joins a gang, wears his colors, takes a spray can and tags his turf, and says, "Here on this street, I'm the man! I can't be the man in a house of my own, with a wife, providing for my children, but at least I can be the man out here on this street —and nobody better mess with me!"

In most cases, a man's primary and instinctive mission in life is to be a husband and provider. Make a "house-husband" out of him and he can't deal with that. You can get away with it for a short period—to enable your wife to complete a degree, for example—but if you try to install such an arrangement for the long term, you are bound to create problems in the home.

Women, too, are designed and constructed for a specific role. God designed women with something that has come to be called "the nesting instinct." I'm sure that, way back at the beginning of history, some guy drove a bear out of a cave, then turned around and said, "Here you are, honey! Your brand-new home!" And the woman followed him into the cave, took a good look around, then said, "I think that rock would look better over there." Pretty soon, she had her husband rearranging rocks and moving bones around until she got the place livable. That's the nesting instinct at work.

Obviously, there are exceptions to all these generalizations I'm making about the sexes. But on the whole, women tend to expend their creativity in making their homes livable, comfortable, and beautiful. In fact, some wives, when they go to a hotel room, will take flowers and pictures from home to make it look less like the Holiday Inn and more like home. If they have to stay in a hotel room for more than a few days, they will even begin rearranging the furniture. Now, I could stay in the same hotel room for a week and it would never occur to me to move more than the remote control, much less a chair or a lamp! I just wasn't created with a nesting instinct.

There are some strong distinctions between husbands and wives that must be taken into account when marriage roles are negotiated. If the husband and wife sit down and agree that it can work for her to take the vice president of marketing job, with all the advantages and liabilities that job will entail, then that's fine. Both partners need to recognize that this means she will come home tired at night, he will have to pick up some of the slack in household maintenance, there might be more "not-tonight-honey" interruptions in their conjugal relationship. All of these issues must be resolved to the satisfaction of both partners.

In 1979, Great Britain elected the first woman prime minister in European history. Shortly after Britain's "iron lady," Margaret Thatcher, moved into No. 10 Downing Street, her husband, Denis, was interviewed by reporters. Predictably, he was asked, "Mr. Thatcher, who wears the pants in your house?"

"I do," Mr. Thatcher replied with a wink. "I also wash and iron them."

A lot of men would not find it easy to keep their sense of humor in the shadow of a woman like Maggie Thatcher. A lot of feminists would say that's a defect in men—"the fragile male ego," they call it. I'm convinced it's not a defect; it's part of man's design to be the strong protector and provider. If the Thatchers were able to successfully negotiate their respective roles, then more power to 'em. Just keep in mind that it's not the norm.

While a husband and a wife are equal co-sovereigns in a marriage, they each have their own role to play. As sovereigns, we have enormous freedom to experiment with those roles, to negotiate and renegotiate those roles, to create the kind of marriage partnership that works most effectively in a given situation. Whatever the arrangement, whatever our roles, one thing is certain: The chances of success for that marriage rise significantly if both partners are able to view themselves as servants of one another.

Love and Respect

Marge stands by the big picture window of her living room, arms folded, tapping her foot, waiting for Harry to get home. "Where is that man?" she wonders out loud. "How long does it take to pick up a bag of nails at the hardware store?" Then she sees his car pull into the driveway. Harry gets out and starts to come up the walk. "Finally!" says Marge.

"Yoo-hoo!" calls a singsong voice from across the street. Marge's jaw drops in dismay as she sees Harry's head whip around. There, across the street, is that new neighbor, Miss What's-Her-Name, the one with the wiggly hips and the bleached-blonde hair (to Marge it is a bleach job). "Yoo-hoo! Harry! Could you help me? My car won't start."

Oooooh! That woman! thinks Marge. *Those big doe-eyes and that helpless little pout! And look at Harry! He's practically falling over himself, running to help her!*

Sure enough, Harry is across the street in a flash, grinning, sucking in his belly. He pops the hood and starts tugging at wires and belts, and generally pretending to know what he's doing, while Miss Helpless Bleach-Blonde Doe-Eyes gushes about how nice it is to have a thoughtful, helpful neighbor right across the street. Finally, Harry gets behind the wheel and says, "Here's your problem. You had it in gear. You have to put it in park to start it."

"Silly old me," says Miss Helpless, fluttering her lashes. "I don't know the first thing about cars! I don't know how I can thank you enough!"

As Harry stands there grinning (he almost forgets to suck in his belly), Marge watches from her living room window—and smoke starts coming out of her ears.

When Harry arrives home, he finds his wife in the middle of the living room, hands on her hips, her eyes shooting laser beams, her jaw as hard the Rock of Gibraltar. "Harold Alfonso Budgeworthy!"

Uh-oh, he thinks. *All three names. I'm in for it now!*

"How dare you rush over there to help that—that woman," she hisses, "while leaving me here to move the refrigerator all by myself!"

Now, this scene is of course a caricature of the kind of scene that is played out in hundreds of marriages every day. So many wives complain that their husbands won't lift a finger to help around the house. Or they ask their husband for help with this or that chore, and he says, "Well, I'll get it in a minute," and two hours later he still hasn't done it. Yet if some shrinking violet from across the street says, "Yoo-hoo!" he'll pull himself away from the Superbowl, make a complete fool of himself, and even give himself a hernia helping her out.

Now, maybe old Harry and a lot of guys like him are not the most sensitive individuals in the world. They don't tune in to their wives' feelings and needs very well. They could use a bit of consciousness-raising.

But in many of these cases, the wives contribute to their own frustration by communicating to the man that he's not really important or respected. He comes home and his wife conveys to him, either subtly or in so many words, "You may be a big shot at the office, but not around here!"

Many wives fail to understand that a man needs to be respected. That is how he is designed by God. A man's role is to exercise dominion, provide leadership and guardianship, and receive respect. If a husband doesn't receive respect at home, then the moment he finds somebody who seems to respect him as a man, *snap*! His head immediately turns in that direction.

Proverbs 31:11 tells us that when a husband's heart safely trusts his wife, then he has "no lack of gain" (or, as the King James Version puts it, "no need of spoil"). A man who has the respect and devotion of his wife does not need to go looking any farther for either honest gain or dishonest gain. He doesn't have to become a workaholic, staying at the office till all hours, pursuing the almighty dollar in order to avoid being home at night. He doesn't have to roam around, looking for another woman to spend his time with. He doesn't have to seek out a companion to pour out his troubles to: "My wife is such a nag, she just doesn't understand me, she doesn't respect me." But if the respect and the trust aren't there, then the man's heart doesn't rest confidently in his wife—and he is more likely to seek his spoil where he has no business seeking it.

Now, I want to make it clear that nothing excuses any husband who behaves irresponsibly or unlovingly toward his wife. The point is that a marriage functions much more smoothly, harmoniously, and happily if *both* partners follow the biblical prescription for marriage. And the biblical prescription is this: Wives are to *respect* their husbands; husbands are to *love* their wives. In Ephesians 5, Paul writes:

> Wives, submit to your own husbands, as to the Lord. For the husband is head of the wife, as also Christ is head of the church; and He is the Savior of the body. Therefore, just as the church is subject to Christ, so let the wives be to their own husbands in everything.
>
> Husbands, love your wives, just as Christ also loved the church and gave Himself for her, that He might sanctify and cleanse her with the washing of water by the word, that He might present her to Himself a glorious church, not having spot or wrinkle or any such thing, but that she should be holy and without blemish. So husbands ought to love their own wives as their own bodies; he who loves his wife loves himself. . . .
>
> Let each one of you in particular so love his own wife as himself, and let the wife see that she respects her husband (Eph. 5:22–28, 33).

The Bible says several times, "Husbands, love your wives." But he never says, "Wives, love your husbands." To the wives, he says, "Let the wife see that she respects her husband." That is, she is to regard him, honor him, venerate him, esteem him, defer to him, praise him, and admire him. Why does Paul give different instructions to husbands and wives? Because women need love and men require respect. It is part of a man's design to require respect. That is why a man will bristle and fight whenever he feels his sovereignty and his manhood have been disrespected. But a man cannot be what God designed him to be as a husband and father without respect. Respect turns a man's head; romance turns a wife's.

How God Views Marriage

As you read what Scripture has to say about marriage, you see again and again that it is seen as a deep and mystical union which symbolizes the relationship between Christ and the church. The biblical argument weaves in and out, first talking about the husband-and-wife relationship, then about the relationship between Christ and His church, back and forth, back and forth. Ephesians 5 concludes with a quote from Genesis 2:24: "For this reason a man shall leave his father and mother and be joined to his wife, and the two shall become one flesh." Then he adds, "This is a great mystery, but I speak concerning Christ and the church" (Eph. 5:31, 32).

In the apostle Paul's mind, as he writes under the inspiration of the Holy Spirit, it is impossible to separate (a) the marriage relationship between man and woman from (b) the marriage relationship between Christ and church. The husband is given an example of love: Christ loved the church and gave Himself for the church—and husbands should love their wives in the same way. If you are a Christian husband or a young man contemplating marriage, roll this thought over in your mind: As a husband, *you stand in the place of Christ* in relationship to your wife. She stands in the place of the church. When you stand at the altar at the side of your bride, one sovereign individual about to freely and volitionally join himself to another sovereign individual, you are asked to make a binding, life-long covenant—a covenant that will be sealed in blood.

Do you take this woman? "I do."

Will you love her? "I will."

Cherish her? "Always."

In sickness and in health? "Absolutely."

In good times and bad? "Without fail."

Will you forsake all others and cleave only to this one woman? "No question."

As long as you both shall live? "Even longer!"

If you are a man in Christ, if you keep that commitment, and if you live out that relationship throughout all the years that God gives you with that woman, then I guarantee you this: You will have an absolutely thrilling, living, growing, pulse-pounding life ahead of you. There will be joys ahead of you that you can't even imagine. You'll be living out the same fascinating adventure with your wife that Christ has planned to live out with His beloved church.

In the same way, the relationship between Christ and the church is to be an example to wives. Christ is the head of the church, and the church owes respect to Christ. In the same way, the husband is the head of the wife, and the wife is to be submissive and respectful to her husband. That doesn't mean you are a doormat, allowing your husband to wipe his dirty feet on you. There are situations where you as a wife should not just blindly submit to your husband—situations such as:

- If your husband abuses you—real abuse, not "incompatible" toilet-seat up abuse;
- If your husband abuses your children, especially physically or sexually;
- If your husband is unfaithful to you, engaging in either heterosexual or homosexual adultery, particularly in an ongoing and unrepentant way;

- If your husband tries to make you engage in any kind of behavior which violates your moral principles and your faith; and
- If your husband tries to make you engage in illegal, destructive, or self-destructive behavior.

In any of these situations, you need counsel from an informed pastor or a qualified Christian counselor. If there is life-threatening violence involved in your situation, you should *immediately* remove yourself and your children from that situation and seek help.

The Key to a Good Marriage: Total Surrender

When I was taking karate, one of the first things we learned was that karate involves not just the ability to fight and defend oneself. It also involves an attitude of respect and courtesy toward others, including opponents. This attitude is demonstrated by bowing—and there are two ways to bow. When you bow to an equal—an opponent or another student—you bow with your head up, looking directly at him. You are saying, *We are equals. If you try anything, I am capable of defending myself against you.*

However, when you bow to the sensei, the martial arts master, you bow with your head down and your eyes to the ground. You are saying, *I am the student, you are the master. I am powerless against you. I am incapable of resisting whatever you would choose to do to me.* Bowing with your head down and eyes lowered is an act of submission.

I've often thought of the profound spiritual and practical lesson exemplified in these two forms of bowing. Who is our Master and Teacher? Jesus Christ. And how do we bow to Him? Do we bow completely, totally, with our eyes to the ground, signalling our complete submission to Him as Lord of our lives? Or do we raise our head, do we look Him in the eyes with a glare of pride?

We have the God-given authority and right to lift our head and glare at Him in defiance. But we should be aware that He is the Master, the Greater Sovereign, and if we declare war on Him, there is no way we can win. Jesus demands—and He pleads—for us to submit our sovereignty to Him. There will be consequences to pay if we do not bow to Him in surrender.

What Christians often fail to understand is that this principle also applies in marriage. When two people mutually submit and surrender to one another, they literally become one flesh. When both sides have surrendered and bowed completely to each other, then neither side has to defend his or her sovereignty. How can my spouse insult my sovereignty when I have already surrendered my sovereignty?

First surrender everything to Jesus and *only* to Jesus. In Christ, I'm able to turn the other cheek. Apart from Christ, I can't turn the other cheek if someone strikes me because I have not submitted my sovereignty to Christ. In fact, it would be absolutely foolish to turn the other cheek apart from Christ, because I have a legal, sovereign right, granted by God Himself, to protect my sovereignty. No one has a right to violate my sovereignty, so I don't have to turn the other cheek if I don't want to.

But once I've submitted and surrendered my sovereignty to the Lord Jesus Christ, then I no longer own my sovereignty; He does. Once I've surrendered to Christ, He becomes my protection. That's what the blood covenant of the cross of Christ does for us. When God came down and made a blood covenant with Abram, He said, "Do not be afraid, Abram. I am your shield, your exceedingly great reward" (Gen. 15:1). *Abraham* (after the covenant) knew he could trust God with every aspect of his life, including his daily protection and daily provision. That's what a covenant does—and it works the same way for you and me today as it did for Abraham.

Here's an important principle to remember about covenants: You should only make covenants with individuals who have the ability to protect your interests. When we make a covenant with God, we know that He has the power to protect us. The Lord Jesus Christ is our shield and our exceedingly great reward. He submitted Himself to the pain and humiliation of the cross, absorbing insults and injuries to His sovereignty that we can scarcely imagine—but He was able to endure it because He had surrendered His sovereignty to the Father. In the same way, we submit ourselves to Christ, surrendering our sovereignty to Him. In doing so, we relinquish our claim on our own sovereignty, so that these insults and injuries that routinely come our way as a part of *any* marriage—including the very *best* marriages—no longer belong to us. They belong to Jesus Christ.

When both partners in a marriage see their goal as complete surrender, then that marriage becomes a thing of unbelievable joy, beauty, and satisfaction. And even if only one partner in the marriage practices this principle of surrender to Christ, it can be a powerful testimony to the unbelieving partner. As Paul writes in 1 Corinthians 7:16, "For how do you know, O wife, whether you will save your husband? Or how do you know, O husband, whether you will save your wife?"

Marriage between Christians should be different from marriage between other people. As Paul says, "No one can say that Jesus is Lord except by the Holy Spirit" (1 Cor. 12:3). When you truly acknowledge the lordship of Jesus Christ, you surrender every vestige of your sovereignty to Him. The extent that you do *not* surrender your sovereignty is the extent to which Jesus is *not* Lord of your life. It's as simple as that. But once you have surrendered all to Him, He becomes the Lord of your life and the Lord of your marriage. He becomes the shield over your marriage, and your exceedingly great reward.

I am convinced that a major cause of tension and conflict in marriages is that many couples have bought into the lie that marriage is a fifty-fifty proposition. As God designed it, marriage is not fifty-fifty, it's 100 percent, it's the whole enchilada. A fifty-fifty proposition is where you split something down the middle and say, "Here's my half and there's your half." But God says the two "shall become one flesh" (Gen. 2:24), a unified whole, without seam or dividing line. A one-flesh union is fully possible only if both partners surrender their sovereignty—first to Christ, and then to one another.

Unfortunately, most couples—including most Christian couples—enter into marriage with an ideal in mind. "This woman is going to make me happy for life!" "This man is going to fulfill my dream of romance and security forever!" But when the ideal crashes against the shoals of reality, they begin to collect insults and injuries against their sovereignty. So there they sit: He waits for her to change, she waits for him to change, both are demanding the 50 percent owed them under the marriage "bargain" they think they've made.

The only solution to this standoff is *total surrender*. Once these two people understand that they must surrender their sovereignty to the Lord Jesus Christ and to each other, they can begin letting go of the "50 percent" they think they are "owed. That's part of the deep mystery of marriage that Paul marvels over in Ephesians 5:32.

King Edward VIII of England (1894–1972) will always be remembered as the man who gave up his throne—his sovereignty as the King of England—for the love of an American woman. After abdicating, he married Wallis Warfield Simpson in France in 1937. He was then given the title of Duke of Windsor. It was a decision he said he never regretted.

Some years after his marriage, the former king was asked how he maintained a good relationship with his wife. "Well," he said with a grin, "I do have an advantage. In a pinch, it helps to be able to remind your bride that you gave up the throne of England for her." Every marriage in the world—including your marriage and mine—could be a stronger, healthier, happier, more satisfying marriage if both partners could say, "I've given up my throne, I've surrendered my sovereignty, I've yielded 100 percent of my expectations and rights and pride to the Lord Jesus Christ."

9

RAISING A SOVEREIGN CHILD

Most of my memories of growing up in a little Texas town are happy memories.

This, however, was the South under segregation, so I went to an all-black, "separate but equal" school. In the back of my mind, I knew that white kids went to a different school, that they had newer textbooks and equipment, but I didn't worry about it or feel bitter about it. I was happy with my school and, it was close: There was nothing but a big field between my back door and the schoolhouse. I think childhood is a lot more miserable in the days of forced busing.

The schoolhouse was a single room, divided in half by a sliding partition. There were two teachers for eight grades. One taught first through fourth grades on one side of the partition, the other taught fifth through eighth grades on the other. They made us read, write, and do research, and when the teacher had assigned one grade to a task, she went on to the next grade and gave those students their assignments. One of those teachers was also the principal—she was my mother.

Momma was a strong, energetic, dedicated woman, full of laughter, rich in faith, with praise for God always on her lips. She had her stern side, too—which no doubt enhanced her effectiveness as a teacher, a principal, and a mother. There are some advantages to having your own mother as your teacher—a sense of familiarity, a comfort zone. But there are also disadvantages. Though I'm aware that childhood perceptions and memories can get a bit distorted, I'm convinced to this day that Momma was tougher on me than on any of the other kids in that school. And I know why.

It's very common in such situations for parents to bend over backwards to show they are not showing favoritism toward their own child. Now, I was no dummy—I did good work and pulled good grades. Problem was, if I did A plus work, she'd only give me an A minus. There was always something subtracted, something taken away, just to make sure there was no suggestion that I was the "teacher's pet." I wanted to excel, to be told what a great job I was doing, yet my best never seemed quite good enough. And I know that this "minus-mark," which was appended to all my efforts, had a deleterious effect on my self-esteem. It didn't destroy me or scar me for life, but it hurt.

It would have helped to have heard once in a while, "Ben, I'm proud of you. Ben, I love you. Ben, you're growing up to be a fine young man."

Grownups—and especially parents—are like mirrors where children look to see their own reflections. They derive their image of who they are and whether or not they have worth from what we tell them and how we act toward them. We have the power to make our kids feel strong and self-directed—and we have the power to make them feel worthless and incompetent. We have the power to enable them to see themselves as *sovereign, decision-able, effective human beings*, made in the image of God. But we also have the power to twist that image in their minds, so that they see themselves as helpless, worthless, and unlovable.

Sovereign Self-esteem

We hear a lot these days about self-esteem. A lot of it, unfortunately, is just plain foolishness.

There are new philosophies and approaches to education, which stress a child's self-esteem over and above that child's ability to read and write. Some schools have completely done away with letter grades and competition in the belief that forcing a child to compete against performance standards or other students might damage his fragile self-esteem! The kids are never told whether they are failing or succeeding. And, of course, when no one is allowed to fail, no one excels or succeeds either! The kids in these schools are tested, and the tests reveal that they have excellent self-esteem—but they can't read, can't write, can't do simple math. Yet they not only feel good about themselves, they feel good about their schoolwork!

No one ever taught us about self-esteem in school, or sent us to the school psychologist for a talk. I mean, *what* school psychologist? Instead, they said, "Get your lessons done. Learn to read. Learn to do math."

Yet there were aspects of myself that I felt very good about. I was aware that I was the top reader in my class, and that there were kids older than me who couldn't read as well as I did. It wasn't an ego-thing that said, "I'm better than those kids." It was a sense of mastery that said, "Here is something that I do exceedingly well." Where did that send my self-esteem? Sky-high!

So it seems to me that the answer to problems of self-esteem is not to make everybody the same or to give kids a false sense of mastery when they are really failing. One answer is to help kids find their unique areas of talent, skill, aptitude, and mastery. Not to impose sameness but to inspire excellence.

One of the by-products of decades of "separate but equal" segregated schools was that it drove down the self-esteem of black kids. Over the years, the black community was told by the experts that the reason for segregated schools was that black kids were intellectually inferior to white kids, and if we put all those black kids in with all these intellectually superior white kids, the black kids would not be able to compete. "This is for your benefit," the white politicians and civic leaders told us. If you tell people a big lie long enough and often enough, they almost invariably pick up a measure of belief in that lie.

I spent my entire childhood and adolescence in segregated schools. Then, straight out of high school, I went into the Air Force. Technical school in the Air Force was my first experience with integrated education—but there's nothing particularly academically challenging about technical school. After I left the Air Force thirteen years later and entered an integrated college, the thought that haunted me was, "Will I be able to keep up with all these white kids?" The fundamental lie of "separate but equal" education had so permeated my thinking that I accepted without much question the "fact" that the white kids around me had an advantage.

Imagine my pleasant surprise when I made the dean's list at a mostly white school! Then I didn't need someone to tell me, "You're an African-American! Be proud of who you are! You are somebody!" The education "experts" take black kids out of the mainstream and put them in courses that have no bearing on their daily lives, teaching them about long-dead African kings to build their self-esteem. But kids don't need to be told about long-dead kings if they can *demonstrate* how good they are to themselves and others by their achievements.

The world has a false view of what self-esteem is all about. But God gives us a true standard for self-esteem, and He points us to the true source of self-esteem. His standard of self-esteem is Himself. He says, "I made you in My own image and likeness. I made you sovereign and decisionable, like Me. That is the source of your greatness as human beings. The more you submit your sovereignty to My will, the more like Me you will become. And the more like Me you become, the greater and more successful you become as a human being."

There are many forces in this world today which seek to destroy our kids' sense of their own God-given sovereignty and greatness as human beings made in God's image. One of the most insidious of these forces is a hideously destructive act which our society has labeled "choice"! Renaming abortion "choice" is like something out of Orwell's *1984*. True choice and decisionability entail *responsibility*; the so-called "choice" of abortion is the worst possible *abdication* of responsibility. Our God-endowed American freedom gives us the right to choose where we will live, what career we will pursue, what goals we will set for our lives, how we will worship—and even, God help us, whether or not we will take an innocent life!

Those of us in my generation have never, for the most part, had to deal with this. Abortion was not only illegal, it was virtually unmentionable and unthinkable in the culture we grew up in! The very thought of killing an innocent unborn child in the womb was as horrific a thought as the ovens of Dachau! Yet today an entire generation, the so-called "Generation X" has grown up with the message of abortion "choice." Today's children have been told by Mother—by the very person God designed to be a child's source of love, warmth, security, and acceptance—

"I only allowed you to live because it was convenient. I could have killed you if I wanted. It is my right!"

How valuable does life seem for a child brought up with this message? Is it any wonder that suicide is the number two killer of teenagers? Or that accidents, often caused by recklessness due to anger or depression, are the number one cause?

Is it any wonder that the alarming rise in child abuse and child murder statistics *precisely coincides* with the legalization of abortion in 1973? It's not hard to imagine an abusive parent thinking, "Why didn't I abort you when I had the chance?" After all, if society says it's okay to kill your children in the womb, why should it not a few hours, weeks, or even years after the child is out of the womb?

When we devalue life in the womb, we devalue *all* of life. When we deface and erase the image of God in the womb, we deface and erase God's image from all of humanity. Accepting our sovereignty as human beings, made in the image and likeness of God, means valuing, defending, and protecting that image as sacred, wherever it is, including within the womb.

As parents, we must teach our children that they are loved and treasured, that whatever our society may say, abortion was never an option for us. We must tell them, over and over, that they are children of a sovereign God, that they bear His image and His sovereign likeness. They are unique and decisionable.

That means we should never say to them, "Why can't you be like your brother? Why can't you be like your sister?" We should say, "You are uniquely *you*, with your own special abilities and God-given gifts. You can do whatever you want to do. Take all that marvelous potential, use it to the maximum, explore the wonders of life, unto the farthest reaches of the possibilities God has in store for you!" A child raised on a steady diet of such messages has

a head start toward realizing the life of sovereign decisionability that God has in mind for him.

———

Dads and Other Heroes

Ray and Francie are at the Food Lion store with their
two kids. Francie is a good mother, she's taught her kids
right, she disciplines appropriately, firmly, and lovingly.
But kids are kids, and today Ray and Francie's two kids
are testing the outer limits of their parent's patience. They
have fought over who should push the cart, they have
knocked over an aisle display of Rice-a-Roni, and now they
are tearing off after each other in the frozen food aisle.
"Ronnie! Ricky! Get back here right now!" calls Francie.

Giggling and punching each other, the two boys hang a
left and roar past the deli section. Mozzarella balls go
flying and bounce along behind them like cello-wrapped
soccer balls.

"Boys!" Francie calls. "I mean it! You stop running and
get back here!"

Another left turn, and the boys are turning cartwheels
past the rows of mayonnaise jars and salad dressing bot-
tles.

"Ronnie!" shouts Francie. "Ricky!" All around the store,
heads turn in Francie's direction.

Laughing, hollering, knocking over little old ladies, the
boys scramble headlong for the produce section.

"Boys," growls a low voice, "stop!"

Two pairs of running shoes, size six and size eight,
screech to a halt.

"Yes, Daddy."

"Okay, Daddy."

Why did Ronnie and Ricky ignore their momma's re-
peated warnings, but snap to attention at a single sentence
from their daddy? Was it because the father is a brutal
ogre? Was it because they were afraid he was going to

beat them? No. Despite politically correct positions to the contrary, I'm convinced that fathers are designed by God to be the natural authority figures in the home.

I can't remember my father ever spanking me. Fact is, my mother did most of the spanking. Yet I regarded my father as the ultimate figure of authority in the household. I would rather risk one of my momma's spankings than one of my daddy's narrow-eyed looks. If he just turned around and looked at me and snapped his fingers, *boom!* My behavior was instantly transformed. It wasn't because my father was a tyrant. He was a very good and loving father, but he was also the unquestioned authority in our home. I respected that authority—and I rarely ever crossed it.

Kids need that kind of security. They need limits and boundaries in order to feel secure, and they look to us, the parents, to set those boundaries. They need someone to be in charge, an example to pattern themselves after, a hero to worship.

To be a hero to your child, you have to spend time with that child. Not just so-called "quality time," but big heaping helpings of time spent together, talking together, playing together, praying together, reading together, shooting baskets together, building a relationship together. Some studies have shown that the average dad spends about two minutes out of every twenty-four hours actually talking with his children—and that usually at the child's insistence. You can't become a hero to your child if your child sees more of "who's hot" than he sees of you.

There is a lot being written and said these days about the importance of mothers, and the role mothers play in the development of a child's personality and emotional makeup. Without question, the mother's role is critical. However, there is a lot less being written and said about the importance of fathers. This is tragic, because kids need both a mother and a father. God designed the family to provide children with both a softer, gentler, nurturing, comforting parent (Mother) and a stronger, firmer, guiding, disciplining parent (Father).

When a child falls off his bike and bumps his head, does he run into the house wailing for Daddy? Of course not! An injured child knows that if he runs to Daddy, Daddy will say, "Lemme see your head, boy. What are you crying for? It's not bleeding much! It's just a little gash! Run in the house and have Momma wash it out!"

That's not what this child is looking for! He wants sympathy and comforting. He wants to be babied! And that's okay! Children need the warm, soothing ministrations of a mother, balanced by the stability, strength, and discipline of a father. Certainly, there are situations where it is impossible for a child to have two parents, and in those situations one parent must do the best he or she can, with help of God, to give that child both the nurturing and the disciplining that is needed.

Boys need a father as a role model, so that they can know what true godly manhood is all about. Boys need a father's embrace, his "rassling" and roughhouse play, his encouragement, his words of guidance, his straight-on look in the eye that says, "You're my son and I'm proud of you!" Some fathers are afraid to touch and embrace their sons, saying, "I don't want him to turn into the kind of boy who likes other boys!" Fact is, studies show that homosexuality is more likely to occur in boys who have distant, non-affectionate, non-touching fathers. Lacking the affirmation and affection of their own fathers, these boys sometimes turn to sexual relationships with other men in a misguided search for the honest masculine relationship they never had with Dad.

Girls, too, need the disciplined love and strength of a father. They need to hear their fathers say, "You are valuable, you are special, you are lovely." When girls reach adolescence without receiving the love they require from their fathers, they go out into the streets to find it. Many girls become pregnant or contract sexually transmitted diseases in a vain search for a substitute father-love. A girl needs a sense of acceptance, a sense of specialness, a hug from the most important man in her life. If she doesn't receive it from Daddy, she figures, "There must be something wrong with me. I must not be pretty, witty, bright, or sexy. I must be lacking in something, or my daddy would love me." Soon, a boy comes along and says, "There's nothing wrong with you, baby! I love you! Let me show you how much I love you!" And she falls into his hands like a ripe peach from a tree.

A father's love helps both sons and daughters to recognize their own sovereign worth and decisionability, in order for them to make consistently healthy moral choices. A father reinforces a child's sense of self-worth, and fortifies a child's moral values. The child who feels secure and valued is far less likely to succumb to moral temptation than the child who has holes of emotional emptiness in his or her personality.

Principle Versus Procedure

Children want and need a clearly defined moral framework in which to learn and grow. They need to gradually gain experience in exercising their sovereign decisionability. Children are like kites on the wind. We gradually let out more and more line, gradually give them more and more freedom, allowing them to soar higher and freer.

As our children mature, we instill in them a core of healthy, moral principles which gradually solidify a moral pillar called character. The more firm the inner framework of principles inside them, the less they need the artificial, outer structure of legalism and rules to control their behavior. Our job as parents is not to bind up our children with a lot of laws and regulations, but to enable them to make good sovereign choices.

One of the ways we build healthy, godly principles in our children's lives is by teaching them the difference between *principles* and *procedures.* A principle is a settled conviction which guides your life. A procedure is a policy or method designed to help life move along smoothly. In parent-child relationships, there should be room for flexibility and compromise—but keep one thing in mind: Compromise only on procedure, never on principle. If we get confused about principle and procedure, the result is confusion, hurt, and conflict, both in families and individuals.

Kids require and desire consistency. They're quick to nail you with the argument, "You said this or did this yesterday, and now you're saying no!" The answer to this problem is to (1) make sure you are consistent and unbending in matters of principle, and (2) communicate to your children that, from time to time, it's okay to be flexible on procedure.

Here's an example of a principle: *It is always wrong to lie.* So we tell our kids, "Never lie to me. This is not a matter for compromise or flexibility. Always, always, always be truthful."

Here's an example of a procedure: *You are always to be home by 10 o'clock on a Friday night.* Sometimes, if there's a special concert or if there's a New Year's Eve party at church or some other special circumstance, you can bend that procedure so that the child can stay out till a mutually agreed-upon time. A family curfew is not a moral principle, it's procedural, one of the rules of the house—and it should have a measure of elasticity.

When kids understand the difference between a principle and a procedure, they are better able to make good choices. A common problem is for a teenager to break curfew, showing up at 11:00 P.M. instead of 10:00 P.M. If that teenager has a solid foundation of uncompromising principle at the core of his personality, he will say, "Mom, Dad, I'm sorry, I was hanging out with the guys and I completely forgot about the time. As soon as I looked up and saw the time, I came right home." As a parent, you may decide to let one infraction slide or to impose a light penalty. It was a breaking of procedure, not principle, and while it is punishable, it is not as extreme as a violation of principle would be.

But if that kid comes home and hands you a whopper, he has just whipped the tar out of a settled, inviolable principle: "Thou shalt not lie, kid!" That child needs to know that he would have been far better off to take his medicine for fracturing procedure than to shatter principle.

In our family, we established the Ten Commandments as our set of moral principles. Honor God; that's first and foremost. Honor your parents; disrespect for parents and other adults is never allowed, no exceptions. Do not steal; it doesn't matter if you were broke or hungry, or if you were "only" stealing a piece of gum, stealing is always wrong. Do not lie; this is not negotiable. These are all examples of principles, and we don't compromise on principles.

It's actually healthy to negotiate changes in family procedures from time to time. People and situations change, and procedures need to adjust to these changes. When kids understand they live under an umbrella of nonnegotiable principles and negotiable procedures, conflict is reduced, life is easier to understand, choices are clearer, and they gradually become wiser and more capable of handling and using their sovereign decisionability.

All principles should apply equally to Mom, Dad, kids, and even grandparents. Problems will sometimes arise when Grandma and Grandpa come into the home and violate some of the rules of the house. This can create conflict between parents and kids, between Mom and Dad, between parents and grandparents. One way this conflict can be eased and resolved is by differentiating between principles and procedures.

If Grandma and Grandpa want to bend one of the family procedures—by, say, keeping the kids up past their normal bedtime or feeding them more sweets than they are usually allowed—there may well be some room to flex the rules a bit. But if Grandma or Grandpa suggests to the kids that it's okay to break a moral principle, the brakes have to be applied, hard and fast: "This is our house and these are our kids, and these are our principles. We don't compromise principle around here."

One of the most important lessons children must learn: *All actions have consequences*. This lesson is lost on many segments of our society, and in many families today. No matter how innocuous the matter may seem on the surface, it should be used as a teaching opportunity so that the child will learn that every action has a consequence. If you discover that your child has stolen a candy bar from the drug store, you should not simply pass that off with a "don't ever do that again." The child needs to understand that he has violated a moral principle, and there is a price to pay. The child should be taken back to the store and face the man at the counter and say, "Sir, I stole this from your store, and I'm returning it (or the money for it). I'm really sorry, and I'm asking you not to press charges. I promise I'll never do this again."

The principles we teach our children with our words must be backed up with our lives. We tell them, "Be honest, don't lie, be consistent." But then our kids catch us in lies and hypocritical behavior. A common example: the way we talk about others. We should never say anything about Mr. and Mrs. Smith in the presence of our children that we are not prepared to say in the presence of Mr. and Mrs. Smith. If we have two different faces in our dealings with people, we are promoting dishonesty and hypocrisy in our children. No matter how embarrassing or unpleasant it may be, children should understand that Mom and Dad always tell the truth.

Children will sometimes gripe and say, "I don't want to go to school! School is stupid! My teacher's a jerk!" Now, where would a kid get an idea like that? Often, he gets it from hearing Mom or Dad say, "I hate this stupid job! My company's just ripping me off, and my boss is an idiot!" Instead of griping about feeling trapped in a "stupid" job, we should use this situation as an opportunity to teach our kids about our own sovereign decisionability.

If you don't like your job, acknowledge the fact that you have choices. Then find a job you do like and get on it! Until then, give your current job your very best effort—and let your kids know what you are doing: You are making sovereign choices in order to build a better life for yourself and your kids. By doing so, you raise children who are prepared to make choices and positive changes in their own lives.

Richard was in a car with three of his friends after a chaperoned party. Richard's friend Jason was driving. "Man," said Jason, "that party was really lame. I didn't have any fun at all. Let's have a blast!" Jason stopped at a convenience store and left the motor running.

Inside the store, Jason put a few six-packs of malt liquor on the counter, produced a fake I.D., and paid for the stuff. In the car, the liquor was passed around and opened. A can was shoved in Richard's hand. He felt the other guys watching him to see what he would do. He fingered the tab, wobbling between two choices.

Jason put the car in gear, and urged it out of the parking lot and onto the street.

"Hold it!" said Richard. "Let me out!"

"Oh, man!" groaned Jason. "Don't wimp out on us, Rich!"

"Just stop the car and let me out!" insisted Richard. He tossed the can in the front seat. "Stop the car *now*!"

The car squealed to a stop at the curb, and Richard jumped out. Then the car sped away. Richard walked back to the convenience store, put a quarter in the pay phone, and punched in his own phone number. His dad answered.

"Dad," said Richard, "I'm at the Seven-Eleven on Brice and J Street. I need a ride."

"Wait inside the store, son. I'll be there in ten minutes."

No recriminations. No criticisms. Richard's father had an understanding with his son that if he was ever in a critical situation, all he had to do was make a phone call, and Dad would be there, no questions asked. Yes, they would discuss it and resolve it at home, but Dad would listen, and he would understand. He would not jump all over Richard without first hearing the matter. If they had not had such an understanding, Richard might well have taken that drink. Instead, he was able to make a healthy, moral choice. He was able to exercise his sovereign decisionability in a righteous way, because he knew that his parents were there to back him and support him, no matter what situation he faced.

"Train up a child in the way he should go," says Proverbs 22:6, "and when he is old he will not depart from it." If you bend a young sapling in a given direction, then come back ten or fifteen years later, you will find a tree bent over in that same direction. That is why children of abusive parents so often become abusers themselves. That is why children of rigid, legalistic parents often grow up to become rigid, legalistic parents themselves. That is why children who are loved tend to become loving, nurturing adults. If we want our kids to grow up to become secure, wise, decisionable individuals with a full awareness and possession of their own God-given sovereignty, we must begin right now to teach them how to make good choices. Our goal should be to give them a solid foundation of unchanging moral principles, and surround them with the stable-yet-flexible framework of negotiable procedures.

There is a young lady—we'll call her Charity—who was continually getting ragged by her friends about the fact that she was a virgin. Unfortunately, this is not an unusual situation for a sixteen-year-old girl today. Some, if they do not have a strong set of moral principles and convictions, will simply surrender to that pressure. I've heard girls say, "I went ahead and had sex just to get it over with." Charity was not about to surrender to the pressure.

Finally, she had enough. A group of girls were around her, riding her about being a virgin. "Hold it," she said. "Let me tell you something. Any day of the week I choose, I can become just like any of you. But none of you can ever be like me again." Speechless, the other girls turned and, one by one, they drifted away. That was the last time Charity was ever ragged about her virginity.

Children *need* moral principles and they *want* moral principles. A strong moral foundation is the key to raising children to become sovereign, decisionable individuals.

Love Covers a Multitude of Mistakes

I've never made mistakes with my children. I'm sure you have not. Not true. Every parent does. But that doesn't mean our children are scarred for life.

"Love," says 1 Peter 4:8, "will cover a multitude of sins." And it is comforting for parents to know that love also covers a multitude of parental mistakes. When I say "love," I'm not talking gooey, syrupy, sentimental "sloppy agape," but genuine, God-inspired love, aimed at the good of the other person—tough love, if necessary. When our heart's desire is to do what is best and most constructive in the lives of our kids, our love can override even our mistakes and failures as parents.

Many parents today are paralyzed by the thought that they are not parenting correctly according to this book or that talk-show expert. Parents need to relax in their role as parents. If parents truly love their kids and have their children's ultimate best as their aim, God will take up the slack and the kids will generally turn out all right.

I'm not saying we don't have good things to learn from child psychologists and other experts. But the fact is that there are many parents who have never heard of child psychology, who have never read a book by Dr. Spock, and who have managed to raise good children. Some of these parents might have done certain things in raising their children that would have scandalized the experts— but they did it out of love, and their kids sensed the love despite the "wrongness" of the technique.

Most people are better parents than they think. Unfortunately, too many people are afraid of their natural parenting skills, their natural reactions and responses. They are afraid to express motherly love or fatherly, righteous indignation, because they have been conditioned by a bunch of "experts" on "Oprah"—experts who sound wise and knowledgeable, but who have little or no concept of godly principles. They say, "If you don't operate according to this procedure or use that technique, if you spank your child or repress your child's emotional expressiveness, you're not a good parent." Well, that's just not true!

God has equipped you to be a good parent. If you are motivated by love and a sincere desire for your child's well-being, then relax and enjoy the parental role. Parenting is a responsibility—a serious and challenging one— but parenting should also be fun! Love your kids. Enjoy these little independent sovereigns God has entrusted to you. Get in there, ask God to help you, and just be a loving parent to that child—and that will be enough!

In the next chapter, we will see how the amazing truth of our God-given sovereignty affects another kind of "family" relationship—our relationship with our brothers and sisters in the "family of faith," the church.

10

A FELLOWSHIP OF SOVEREIGNS

Several years ago, I was invited to speak at a large Christian convention in Pennsylvania. There were many other speakers at this gathering—several well-known television evangelists and Christian authors. After one session, my friend John Gilman and I were talking with several of the other speakers when a woman came dashing up to us, looking very excited and out of breath. She was waving a big autograph book.

She rushed around to each of us, and we all signed the lady's book. Finally she came to my friend John, who was an executive producer at CBN, and she breathlessly asked, "Are you anybody?"

John shook his head. "No ma'am, I'm not."

Instantly, the woman whirled about and ran off, autograph book in hand, in search of someone who "is somebody."

I think a lot of Christians make the mistake of dividing the church into "somebodies" and "everybody else." While we wouldn't exactly go so far as to say that a fellow

Christian is a "nobody," we do tend to elevate some and minimize the importance of others.

But Jesus doesn't tolerate that kind of thinking. He rebukes it right off. In Luke 9, Jesus catches His disciples arguing among themselves as to which of them would be the greatest. So He brings a child before them and says, in effect, "You should be ashamed of yourselves, arguing about who is the greatest! See this little child? If you want to be great, then get all that nonsense about political power and ruling kingdoms out of your head. Instead, receive the kingdom as this little child, without guile, without agenda, without hypocrisy. Set your sights on being a servant to the least among you instead of on being a ruler and a boss. It's the one who chooses to be the least among you who will be great in the kingdom of heaven." (See Luke 9:46–48.)

Like us, these guys were a hard-headed bunch—so Jesus often had to teach them the same lesson again and again. Just a short time later, in Luke 22, the disciples are having the *same argument* all over again! "I'm gonna be the greatest!" "No, I *am*!" "No, *I* am!" And while the disciples are one-upping each other and puffing themselves up and trash-talking one another, Jesus looks at them sorrowfully—and perhaps a little angrily—and says,

> The kings of the Gentiles exercise lordship over them, and those who exercise authority over them are called "benefactors." But not so among you; on the contrary, he who is greatest among you, let him be as the younger, and he who governs as he who serves. For who is greater, he who sits at the table, or he who serves? Is it not he who sits at the table? Yet I am among you as the One who serves (Luke 22:25–27).

John's gospel records that Jesus also set a powerful, visible example for His disciples. He took a towel and a basin, then went man to man, washing each one's feet, demonstrating to all of them that the Master is a servant! He taught them that the essential question of true Christianity is not, "Who is the greatest?" but, "Who is willing to stoop down and wash feet?"

Who will be the greatest saints in heaven? Somehow, I don't think it's going to be us Christian TV personalities and authors whose autographs are sought. I'm not denigrating or disparaging the faith and service of the Pat Robertsons, the Billy Grahams, and the many other ministers whose books and TV programs are available worldwide. But I do believe that the Lord has some very special rewards planned for those humble Christian men and women who stand behind the scenes, doing unseen acts of generosity and witnessing, living out their faith with courage and boldness, yet who are completely unrecognized and unheralded in this world.

I can just see the headlines in *The Heavenly Gazette*. If Ben Kinchlow wrote a best-seller, visited forty countries, and appeared on all four networks in one day, the story would appear in section D, page 8, column 3. But the front-page banner headline would read, "Mamie Snodgrass Prays in Closet, Pulls Down Enemy Stronghold!"

Reverence for One Another

Because I am made in the image of a sovereign God, I am an immortal sovereign. So are you. So is the next person, and the next, and the next. We are all sovereign, we are all equal, in God's sight. If I understand who I am and who you are—that we are sovereign beings made in the image of the living Lord, the great I AM—then we have the basis of a deep respect for one another, and of a bonded relationship with one another.

It all starts with an intense, committed love for God. As

Jesus said, the greatest commandment is, " 'You shall love the LORD your God with all your heart, with all your soul, and with all your mind.' This is the first and great commandment" (Matt. 22:37–38).

Jesus continues: "And the second is like it: 'You shall love your neighbor *as yourself*' " (Matt. 22:39 emphasis added). You must understand who you are. You need an appreciation for this incredible sovereignty that God has lovingly poured into human flesh. This gives us a solid foundation for healthy, godly self-love and self-esteem. If you can't love yourself, soberly and realistically, then you can't adequately love your neighbor.

Clearly, there is no room in the Christian life for arrogance and self-willed pride. As Paul says, we should take care not to think of ourselves "more highly than [we] ought to think, but to think soberly" (Rom. 12:3). The image of God within us levels the playing field: I am a sovereign being, but no more or less sovereign than anyone else. We are *all* sovereign! In the image of God, we find not only the source of a healthy self-esteem but of a godly sense of humility.

This is where the church should stand out clearly from the rest of society. God designed the church to be a place where people would demonstrate a lavish, extravagant love and regard for one another. Every Christian is expected to say, "It is no longer I who lives, but Christ who lives in me. And Christ lives in every other church member, too. We are all sovereign members of the body of Christ, and none is more important than the other."

But is that the attitude most of us have as Christians? Hardly! We give reverence to those such as "the Right Reverend Bishop Thomas Highpockets" who we think is so high above us mere mortals. Yet we disregard the "ordinary" Christians around us. If only every person had the perspective of C.S. Lewis, who wrote,

There are no *ordinary* people. You have never talked to a mere mortal. Nations, cultures, arts, civilization—these are mortal, and their life is to ours as the life of a gnat. But it is immortals whom we joke with, work with, marry, snub, and exploit. (C.S. Lewis, *The Weight of Glory,* Grand Rapids: Eerdmans, 1965).

And there is a *holiness* about every human being, because every human being bears the stamp of God's likeness. As Lewis goes on to say, this human holiness is magnified in our fellow Christians, because Christ Himself lives within us, and we should have a special reverence for the living Lord who indwells our brothers and sisters in the church.

That's why the Bible refers to the church as "the body of Christ." The church is not just a collection of individuals. It is a single body, and each member of the body is a unique expression of some aspect of the entire body and life of the Lord Jesus Christ. No one is more important than anyone else, and no one is the same as anyone else. We are all uniquely special. We are not all noses or eyes or hands or feet. We are uniquely ourselves, and we are an intricately interconnected part of one another. Those among us who seem less presentable should be covered with honor so that the whole body is equally honored. As Paul writes,

> But God composed the body, having given greater honor to that part which lacks it, that there should be no schism in the body, but that the members should have the same care for one another (1 Cor. 12:24–25).

So we must treat each other with honor in the body of Christ. We must love the Lord our God with all our heart, soul, strength, and mind—and we must love one another in the same way and to the same degree as we love ourselves.(See Luke 10:27.) That means there is no room in the church for favoritism and partiality. As James tells us,

> My brethren, do not hold the faith of our Lord Jesus Christ, the Lord of glory, with partiality. For if there should come into your assembly a man with gold rings, in fine apparel, and there should also come in a poor man in filthy clothes, and you pay attention to the one wearing the fine clothes and say to him, "You sit here in a good place," and say to the poor man, "You stand there," or, "Sit here at my footstool," have you not shown partiality among your-selves, and become judges with evil thoughts? (James 2:1–4.)

The Lord wants us to see that there are no "big shots" in His church. There is only one Big Shot and that's the Lord Jesus Christ Himself, and I mean that with all re-spect and reverence.

Fussin' and Fightin' and Feudin'

Ever hear this? "I believe God is in control of every-thing. If He wants this problem solved, He'll solve it."

Saying, "The Lord is in control," is often nothing more or less than "copping out" and making excuses for our own cowardice. Yes, the Lord is ultimately in control of history—but we are responsible for the choices we make. God holds the future, but He does not control our human will. If we choose to go our own senseless, destructive way, He will let us. He will grieve for us, but He will not stop us. When there's war in the church, God calls us to be peacemakers—but if we say "No" to God, if we permit His church to remain divided, then God will permit it too.

God allows us to have our way in the church, just as He allowed Israel to have its way in the Old Testament. As you read through the Old Testament, you have to ask yourself: "Why did God allow the children of Israel to keep committing such seemingly stupid, disobedient, self-destructive actions? Why did He allow them to turn back from the promised land, to worship a golden calf, to turn aside to false gods?" Then, as you read through the New Testament epistles, and as you look around at the church in our own century, you have to ask yourself: "Why does God allow Christians to behave so foolishly, shamefully, and destructively? Why doesn't He exercise His authority and set the church straight? Hey, He's God, right?"

The answer becomes clear once we understand human sovereignty. In order to maintain our status as human beings, made in His image and likeness, He must give us the freedom to make our own choices, make our own mistakes, and commit our own sins. *He will not overrule our sovereign will, even when the result brings harm to other people and to His church.*

"But," you might say, "God is a loving Father! As a parent, I would never allow my child to play in traffic just to protect his sovereignty! I would correct him, yank him out of the street, even rap him one to help him remember to stay out of traffic! If you love a child, you correct him! You don't just let him do whatever he wants!"

There is some validity to that objection. But just try that when your child is 25 or 35 years old! Yes, we are God's children, He is our loving Father, and the Scriptures teach that He chastens and corrects those whom He loves. But the child-Father analogy only goes so far. We must move beyond childishness and into full maturity, taking hold of our sovereignty, accepting both the freedom and the responsibility that comes with it. He loves us and corrects us as His children. But He also respects our adult sovereignty.

Our God-given sovereignty explains why God was so patient with Israel, and why He continues to be so patient with His erring, defection-prone church. God doesn't stop people—even *Christian* people—from making a mess of things, from hurting other people, and even from hurting the cause of Christ. We have a sovereign right to say "No" to God's plans and commands, and He will not abrogate that right even to further the ministry of His church.

Why is there so much fussin' and fightin' and feudin' in so many churches? Because we get our priorities turned around, and we begin focusing on the wrong things. Jesus told us that our first priority is to seek the kingdom of God and His righteousness. (See Matt. 6:33.) If we would understand that and do that, almost everything else including our problems and differences with our brothers and sisters in Christ is academic.

When we Christians fight, we always fight for the loftiest of reasons—or so we think: "I'm contending for purity of doctrine." "I'm fighting to defend an important ministry." "I'm fighting to defend biblical truth." Somehow, we lose sight of the fact that one of the most important things to be defended in the church is the unity of the Spirit. Just before going to the cross, Jesus knelt in the garden and prayed for His followers, and for generations of followers to come, including you and me. His prayer for the church was "that they all may be one, as You, Father, are in Me, and I in You; that they also may be one in Us, that the world may believe that You sent Me" (John 17:21).

Jesus is saying here that our Christian unity is our witness to the world of the reality of God and His love. As someone once said, "Our oneness is our witness." Keep in mind, however, that unity is not necessarily conformity. There is one Lord, one faith, one baptism, but there is room for diversity and more than one opinion on secondary issues, *if* we cover our differences with Christian love.

When the apostle Paul heard about the divisions and arguments that split the Corinthian church, he immediately wrote to them, saying,

Now I plead with you, brethren, by the name of our Lord Jesus Christ, that you all speak the same thing, and that there be no divisions among you, but that you be perfectly joined together in the same mind and in the same judgment. For it has been declared to me concerning you, my brethren, by those of Chloe's household, that there are contentions among you. Now I say this, that each of you says, "I am of Paul," or "I am of Apollos," or "I am of Cephas," or "I am of Christ." Is Christ divided? Was Paul crucified for you? Or were you baptized in the name of Paul? . . .

Therefore let no one boast in men. For all things are yours: whether Paul or Apollos or Cephas, or the world or life or death, or things present or things to come—all are yours. And you are Christ's, and Christ is God's (1 Cor. 1:10–12; 3:21–23).

What is Paul saying? In updated terms, his message to the conflict-torn Corinthian church is, "Knock it off! How can you guys waste so much time and emotional energy arguing over who follows a greater leader? Our leader is Christ, not Paul or any other mere mortal—and Christ is not divided! So stop bickering about who's the most important man of God. Give me a break! Paul, Apollos, and Cephas (Peter) are just human servants, and belong to you! In fact, the whole world belongs to you! The future is yours! The past is yours! So forget your fears and worries about the future, about life and death and divisions and all that other stuff! Shred the past, and don't let it hold you down! It all belongs to you, and you belong to Christ, and Christ belongs to God!"

The Bible is a book about relationships. God created the human race in order to have someone to have a relationship with—someone made in His own image and likeness. When Adam sinned and the human race fell, that fellowship was broken. Later, God raised up great men and women of faith, people like Abraham, Isaac, Joseph,

Moses, Ruth, Samuel, and David—people who were not "religious," but who had an intense relationship with a living God. When Jesus came to live and die and rise again, He came to restore the broken relationship and re-establish the friendship between human beings and God —and He introduced a new kind of relationship: a caring, honest, love-relationship among brothers and sisters in the body of Christ, the church—a love-relationship called *koinonia*.

Everything Jesus talked about, everything the Bible talks about, centers around fellowship and koinonia relationships. The Christian faith is completely relationship-based. Our Christian relationships in the church grow directly from our relationship with God. It's not what you know, it's who you know. We have good relationships, with good communication and the lavish expression of love and forgiveness in the body—then even the most difficult conditions become bearable. When Christians love one another, they become an irresistible force, even in a climate of persecution, adversity, deprivation, and sorrow.

Joined and Fit Together

When I came to know the Lord in 1970, I hungered for the Word. I was eager to discover all the truth I could about the Lord and His plan for my life. Because I did so much driving, hour after hour on the General Tire test track, I listened to the radio a lot. I was continually twisting the dial, looking for different radio Bible teachers, hungry for every drop of truth I could wring from those airwaves. I even listened to those deep-thicket, pulpit pounding, shouting preachers who would get all wound up and add an extra syllable whenever they said phrases like "washed in the blood-uh" and "born again-uh." There was one radio preacher who was different from the rest, and who was heard on a lot of stations in those days. By flipping from station to station, I could listen to him off and on for almost the whole shift. I was really getting hooked on this guy's message.

I had just started a wear test on the track, which meant I'd be driving one car, eight hours a day, for a full month or two. It was a brand-new Chevrolet with an excellent radio, so I'd really be able to "tune in" to this preacher.

At the same time, however, I didn't want to take just anyone's word as truth. I wanted *the* truth, not just *a* truth. So I prayed, "Lord, I need to know if this guy is legitimate, if the things he says are of You. If You want me to, I'll keep listening to this radio preacher. If not, please show me." The day after I prayed this, I went into the office and routinely checked the board for my car assignment—and I had been switched to a different car: a brand-new Lincoln Continental! You *know* a car like that has to have a great radio! Push buttons, FM stereo, the works!

I went out to the lot, found the Lincoln, slid in behind the seat and—What?! *No radio!*

Well, I drove that Lincoln day after day without any radio to listen to. Two weeks later, I checked the car assignment and found they had put me in a truck. I went out and looked at the truck's dashboard. Again, no radio. I was beginning to get a message. God had answered my prayer. He was telling me, "I don't want you listening to that radio preacher. I want you listening to Me!" (Turned out, it was a cult.)

So I began getting deeper and deeper into the Word while spending more time in prayer. That investment of time in prayer and Bible study paid remarkable dividends as I entered full-time ministry. One of the most fascinating studies I did was in Ephesians chapter 4, where I discovered what is called "the five-fold ministry":

And He Himself gave
  some to be apostles,
  some prophets,
  some evangelists,
  and some pastors
  and teachers (Eph. 4:11).

As I studied this passage, the thought came to my mind, *Why? Why did Jesus give these gifts, these ministries, these specially endowed people to His church?* As I read and meditated, I found the answer right in the passage: to prepare God's people! Jesus gave those gifts

for the equipping of the saints for the work of ministry, for the edifying of the body of Christ, till we all come to the unity of the faith and of the knowledge of the Son of God, to a perfect man, to the measure of the stature of the fullness of Christ (Eph. 4:12–13).

I had continually heard sermons preached out of Ephesians 4, and the focus of those sermons had always been on the gifts, the five-fold ministry. The honor was accorded those who were so gifted. But that's not where the focus of the passage is. In this text, the apostle Paul says the function of these gifts is "for the equipping [perfecting] of the saints [ordinary Christians] for the work of the ministry, for the edifying [building up and establishment] of the body of Christ [the church]." The focus of this passage is not on the five-fold ministry but on God's *people*, on preparing His people to do the work of the ministry. The honor is to be accorded the saints. They are the reason for any giftings in the body.

His goal for every Christian is growth and stability, so that His church would be effective and unified. He has given *us* the five-fold ministry, the five-fold gifts, in order to prepare *us*, establish *us*, mature *us*, and bind *us* together in Christian unity. His goal, according to Ephesians 4, is

> that we should no longer be children, tossed to and fro
> and carried about with every wind of doctrine, by the
> trickery of men, in the cunning craftiness of deceitful
> plotting, but, speaking the truth in love, may grow up in all
> things into Him who is the head—Christ—from whom the
> whole body, joined and knit together by what every joint
> supplies, according to the effective working by which
> every part does its share, causes growth of the body for
> the edifying of itself in love (vv. 14–16).

Jesus Christ is building His body, and He wants a body comprised of mature Christians—Christians who are in the process of *reaching toward the measure of the stature of the fullness of Christ!* Think of it! What a destination! The first time I caught a glimpse of this truth, it was like a bolt of lightning, illuminating my mind, shattering my preconceived notions. The church is not just a group of people singing, shouting, or sleeping in a church building, just making noise and going home. (See the author's booklet, *Making Noise and Going Home*, Chesapeake, Vincom Publications, 1990.) What an awesome, inspiring picture of the church and of our place in Christ!

It is therefore a heartbreaking tragedy that so many of us are willing to hack away at this marvelous body God has designed—amputating members, gouging and wounding it, crippling and dismembering it, saying to this brother or that sister, "My church has no need of you! Our church isn't big enough for me and you! Get out! You're not wanted here!" No body can function that way— not the body of Christ, the church, and not a human body. A body is crippled to the exact extent that one part of that body ceases to function.

Take the two fastest men in the world. Both run the

hundred meter dash in 9.9. Both are completely equal in every respect—height, weight, strength, speed, stamina, motivation, and mental preparedness. There is no difference between them. Put them in a race, and the result will be a dead heat, a photo finish.

But what if, just before the big race, one runner walks into a door and stubs his little toe? Suddenly the entire equation is changed! The runner has injured a tiny, insignificant portion of his body—less than one percent of his entire body mass—yet he no longer has a chance of winning the race.

So it is in the church, the body of Christ. We can't afford a stubbed toe or an amputated finger in the body of Christ. Every member matters. Every individual in the body is critically important—as important as every other member.

That was a powerful revelation to me in the first few years of my Christian experience. Years later, I had occasion to preach a series of messages in L.A. after the riots. During that series, truths from Ephesians, Genesis, and elsewhere in the Bible collided and generated the core ideas of this book—ideas such as our human sovereignty, our decisionability, our right to say "No" to God. As this concept was being born inside me, I kept thinking, "Man alive! How did I miss this? It's all right here in the Word! It's all through Genesis and in the Gospels and in Hebrews and in Paul's epistles, plain as day!"

It was clear that the key to pleasing God and living victoriously is *surrender*. Yes, we have the right to declare war on God, if we choose, but that leads only to destruction. If we want to live happy, successful, joy-filled, abundant lives, we must set aside our sovereignty, offering it freely and willingly up to God. What's more, I saw that the key to a successful, joy-filled church is for everyone in the body of Christ, every brother, every sister, every pastor, to surrender first to Christ, and then to mutually surren-

der a measure of their sovereignty to one another! When
all members of the church surrender themselves to one
another, they aren't diminished. They become greater, because the church where Christian love flourishes becomes a dwelling place for God! (See Eph. 2:22.)

Bosses and Servants

In one of the "little letters way in the back of the Bible"
is a character we seldom hear about. Few sermons are
ever preached about him (I've never heard one). Many
Christians have never heard of him. His name is Diotrephes, and we find him in the third epistle of John. Diotrephes is what today we would call a "church boss." Almost every church has at least one "church boss," and
many churches have several. Here's what the apostle
John has to say about "Boss Diotrephes":

> I wrote to the church, but Diotrephes, who loves to have
> the preeminence among them, does not receive us.
> Therefore, if I come, I will call to mind his deeds which he
> does, prating against us with malicious words. And not
> content with that, he himself does not receive the brethren,
> and forbids those who wish to, putting them out of the
> church (3 John 9, 10).

Was Diotrephes a pastor or a layman? We don't know.
What we do know is that in today's church, we can find
"church bosses" like Diotrephes in both the pews and the
pulpits. Wherever you find someone who loves to have
the preeminence in the church, who secretly enjoys being
admired for being so "spiritual," who feels he's entitled to
get his way in the church, either by reason of his office or
his years of service or his fat checkbook, you have found
a modern-day Diotrephes.

Church bosses don't understand that all believers are

equally sovereign. Their attitude is, "I'm sovereign, you're not." That's why church bosses feel justified in (as the apostle John puts it) "prating against" their fellow Christians "with malicious words" and "putting them out of the church." Church bosses can't stand to be contradicted or to have their plans and agendas thwarted, so they will destroy reputations and chase people out of the church— all in the name of "doing the Lord's work"! In short, they use the methods of the world—hidden agendas, secret strategies, intimidation, backstabbing, rumors, character assassination, and political power plays—in order to achieve their "ministry goals."

God did not intend His church to be ruled by the methods and agendas of this world. He has a completely different definition of "leadership" and "rulership."

The church should not be run by the rules of the unbelievers, the rules of this world. Rather, it should operate as the kingdom of God operates. The "constitution" of the kingdom of God is found in what we call the Sermon on the Mount.

This "constitution" begins with a series of seeming contradictions called the Beatitudes: Blessed are the poor in spirit . . . blessed are those who mourn . . . blessed are the meek . . . and on and on, absurdity upon absurdity! This was not what the people were taught then, and it's not what is taught today! Conventional wisdom says that blessing involves riches, success, power, pride, and looking out for Number One! All those things which Jesus calls "blessings" are what this world calls "curses"—poverty, humility, sorrow, righteousness, purity, persecution. This was nonsense in the ears that listened to Jesus on those Galilean hillsides—and it is nonsense in the ears of most people today.

It is here, in the Sermon on the Mount, that Jesus reveals true humility. In 2 Corinthians 10:12, Paul warns us against one of our favorite pastimes: comparing ourselves with other people and saying, "Compared with him, compared with her, I'm not so bad! In fact, I'm doing better than most folks!" That's not the attitude Jesus describes in the Sermon on the Mount. The only valid standard against which to measure ourselves is *God's* standard, the standard of perfection. So the question we must ask ourselves is not, "How am I doing, compared with the next guy?" but, "How am I doing compared to Jesus?"

Whoa! Heavy!

But that's the way to achieve true humility. Jesus said, "Blessed are the poor in spirit," that is, blessed are the humble people. Why? "For theirs is the kingdom of heaven" (Matt. 5:3). That's the requirement for citizenship in the kingdom of heaven: humility.

Jesus goes on: "Blessed are those who mourn, for they shall be comforted." Blessed are those who mourn over *what*? Certainly, those who mourn over losses, pain, and sorrow. But also those who mourn over their own sin and failure, and those who compassionately mourn over the tragedies of others. This doesn't mean Jesus wants us to wear long faces all the time. But He wants us to recognize our true state apart from Him.

"Blessed are the meek," He goes on to say, "for they shall inherit the earth." Meekness is one of the most misunderstood concepts in Scripture. We hear Jesus called "meek and mild," or we hear Swinburne's line, "Thou hast triumphed, O pale Galilean," and we get an almost "nerdy" or "sissy" image of the Lord Jesus Christ. We tend to think of meekness as weakness, and so for centuries Jesus has been portrayed as a thin, mild-mannered, almost effeminate man rather than the strong, muscular, sun-tanned Galilean carpenter He must have been.

We need to understand what true biblical meekness is. We find that word defined in the lives of those whom the Bible calls "meek." Take Moses, for example—a man of boldness and action, who stood toe to toe and eye to eye with the King of Egypt, demanding that the children of Israel be set free. He was a man of physical strength and character strength, calling his people to obedience before God, and confronting them sternly when they strayed, dashing the tablets of the Ten Commandments to pieces, grinding their golden idol into fine powder and forcing the people to drink it! Yet the Bible says of him, "Now the man Moses was very humble [or, in the King James Version, *meek*], more than all men who were on the face of the earth" (Num. 12:3).

And what about Jesus? He boldly stood up to those who wanted to stone Him and kill Him, and walked right through an angry lynch mob. He never backed down from a confrontation. He called the hypocritical religious leaders "snakes" and "tombs full of dead men's bones"—and He said it to their faces! He took a whip and drove the moneychangers out of God's Temple. That doesn't sound like meekness as we usually understand the term—yet Jesus Himself said, "Take my yoke upon you and learn of me; for I am meek and lowly in heart: and ye shall find rest unto your souls" (Matt. 11:29 KJV).

People tend to think, "Oh, he's meek, he never gets mad," or, "She's meek, she would never confront anyone." That's a misunderstanding of what true meekness is. The meek are not people who lack courage and passion. The meek, in a biblical sense, are people who have the ability to *control* and *channel* their passions! The meek know when to get mad, and when to rein in their anger.

True meekness is like a powerful, spirited stallion whose rider is a valiant king. This stallion has submitted his own sovereignty to the king, so when the king says, "Rein in your passions," the stallion pulls up short, and when the king says, "Now! The battle is at hand!" the stallion leaps into action. Those who are in control, and who obey their King in all meekness and humility, will inherit the earth. Those who are out of control and undisciplined in mind, body, and emotions will inherit nothing. Only the meek are fit to lead.

There is so much more that Jesus has to say about the way things work in the kingdom of God. We've examined just a very brief introduction to the "Constitution" of God's Kingdom, which Jesus lays out in detail in the Sermon on the Mount. Here are some of the implications we find in this Sermon:

- **The church must be served with love and righteousness, not ruled with political power.**
- **True rulership is servanthood.**
- **The people we serve as leaders of the church are our peers and equals, not our subjects and inferiors.**

A Witness to the World

The implications of godly servant-leadership in the church reach far beyond the walls of the church and into the nine-to-five marketplace where we live out most of our waking lives. Unfortunately, churches often elect or appoint business leaders to sit on church boards based solely on their secular success, and these business leaders bring worldly business principles into the church. Soon, the church begins to look and function exactly like any other business, and the members of the church begin to feel more like customers than members of a body.

Instead of allowing the world to set the agenda for the church, we should be taking godly, biblical principles into the world and running our secular affairs as God would have us run the church! That means that those of us who are owners, executives, managers, and employers should begin treating our employees as sovereigns, made in the image of God. We need to understand that a worker is not a cog in a money-making machine, nor a galley slave to be flogged and screamed at.

What is an employee? He or she is an immortal sovereign individual who has voluntarily surrendered a measure of his or her God-given sovereignty in exchange for a fair wage. Here, then, is a totally new paradigm for looking at our business life and our employees. You can read all the latest books on re-inventing your corporate culture, on motivating and involving your employees, on team-building and inspiring the troops. Many of these books offer good ideas. But all of these ideas, such as doing away with management's parking slots and executive washrooms, are just so much meaningless window dressing and gimmickry if there is not a genuine shift in the way employers view and relate to their employees.

We must begin to see employees as genuine equals. That doesn't mean we do away with a chain of command, with levels of responsibility and accountability, and turn our businesses into anarchist societies without direction or control. But we must understand that having a more senior rank does not make us more sovereign than the rank-and-file. The guys in the boiler room are every bit the equals of the executive in the corner office. The execs may have specialized knowledge, which qualifies them to work in the front office. But the execs should never forget that they probably don't have the specialized skill to work a lathe with the same skill as the machine worker they hired to do the job.

Who is the better man—the one in the three-piece suit or the one in the blue coveralls? Who is more sovereign? We human beings often get confused on that score—but God never does. There is no partiality with Him.

Servant of the Servants

As executive vice president of Christian Broadcasting Network, my responsibilities included being in charge of "700 Club" counseling centers all across the United States and in several foreign countries. I could call up the individual director of each counseling center and request an accounting of the operations of that center. I could hire those directors, set productivity levels for them, examine the records of how many people and churches were being served, and discharge them if need be.

As I looked at this monumental task, the first question that came to my mind was, "What do I want to achieve?" The answer was clear: *the maximum ministry productivity for the people in need, the callers.* So the next question was, "What can I do to help my staff get the job done, effectively and productively?"

How could I help each one? By communicating with them, meeting with them, listening to them, talking to them. "What I can do to help you meet your goals. How can I serve you?"

In Matthew 8, a Roman centurion comes to Jesus and says, "Lord, my servant is lying at home paralyzed, dreadfully tormented." Now here was a Roman centurion who had, in the course of his duties, ordered men into battle— even to their deaths. But he sees himself not merely as a boss but as a servant to those who serve under him. When his own servant falls ill, this centurion thinks, "I keep hearing about this itinerant rabbi who heals people. I've got to go to Him."

The centurion didn't have to do this. He could have said (as many have done), "I'll just fire this guy and go hire someone who's healthy. If my servant gets better, I may give him his job back, but right now I need a replacement." But he didn't. He chose to serve the servant. He understood the true nature of authority and leadership: It is not about lording it over others, ruling others, and bossing people around. It's about getting the job done, effectively and productively, with compassionate respect for the sovereignty of every person involved.

When the centurion tells Jesus that his servant is ill, Jesus replies, "I will come and heal him." Or perhaps Jesus actually says, "Am I to come and heal him?" There were no question marks in the original Greek language of the New Testament, but I think it is more likely that Jesus put it in the form of a question.

The centurion replies, "Lord, I am not worthy that You should come under my roof. But only speak a word, and my servant will be healed. For I also am a man under authority"—not a man *with* authority, but a man who must answer to others in authority over him—"having soldiers under me. And I say to this one, 'Go,' and he goes; and to another, 'Come,' and he comes; and to my servant, 'Do this,' and he does it."

This centurion recognized that his authority didn't come from being "more sovereign" than anyone else. It came from the fact that he himself was a servant to the one who was in charge over him.

The centurion recognized Jesus as being sent from God, acting with full God-given authority over nature and disease. So when Jesus says, "Well, should I come and heal your servant?" the centurion doesn't say, "Of course! What did you think I came all this way for? Get moving! I'm a Roman centurion, the sovereign boss around here!" No, the centurion says, "I am not worthy that You should come under my roof."

Here is a man who understood authority and human sovereignty—and the humility that rightfully goes with it. He used his own authority with care, respecting the sovereignty of others, rejecting the temptation to use his power to lord it over others. He recognized the authority of Jesus and submitted himself to Jesus with faith in His power and position. Furthermore, he possessed a true understanding of where Jesus derived His rightful authority, He was duly constituted of God. And Jesus marveled at his understanding: "Assuredly," He said, "I say to you, I have not found such great faith, not even in Israel!" (Matt. 8:5–13).

Our God-given sovereignty is the source of so many beautiful paradoxes of faith and Christian living. It is the source of our greatness and our humility. Because we are all immortal and sovereign, we are all equal and deserving of respect.

11

THE ULTIMATE FREEDOM

Back in the early seventies, I served as the director of a Christian drug and alcohol rehab farm in Killeen, Texas. I had never heard of Pat Robertson or "The 700 Club," which at that time was broadcasting on a rotating basis from studios in Atlanta, Dallas, and Portsmouth, Virginia. Unbeknownst to me, the man I worked with, Bob Bearden, called up "The 700 Club" one day, and said, "Listen, next time you do the show in Dallas, you need to get this former black militant on. He got saved a couple years ago, and he's got all kinds of stories about miracles he's seen on this rehab farm he runs."

So they called me up and asked if I'd come down and be on "The 700 Club." I said, "Hey, I'll go anywhere, anytime, anyhow to talk about Jesus!" So I went on the show. I thought it went pretty well. It was a two hour show, and I had a great time with Pat Robertson. It seemed pretty easy to me. Just sit and answer Pat's questions and talk about the miracles I had seen, how I met the Lord, and the lives that were being changed on the rehab farm. I forgot all about the cameras and the audience. When the show was over, that was the end of that, as far as I was concerned.

I went back to work at the drug and alcohol rehab farm, and didn't give any more thought to "The 700 Club." Weeks passed, and then I got a call from Ruth Eggert, the show's guest coordinator. She said, "Would you come and help Pat Robertson do a show?"

In those days, the show was hosted by Pat, co-hosted by Henry Harrison, and a third guy, the local station manager, was in the telephone section. Once or twice in an hour-long segment, Pat would throw it to the phones and say, "What's happening on the phones?" They would share a prayer request or a praise report. So when they asked me to come do "The 700 Club," I thought, "Hey, I can do that!"

So off I went up to Portsmouth, Virginia. Though the main studio in Portsmouth back then was nothing like the CBN facilities we now have in Virginia Beach, it was much larger than the other studio I had visited in Dallas. I thought, *Wow! All these bright lights and cameras moving around, people coming in and taking their seats—this is exciting!*

The show was broadcast live, to three privately owned-and-operated stations and two or three affiliates, and I was standing around, chatting with the telephone counselors, waiting for airtime. I was right there so I would be ready when Pat Robertson would go to the phones. With just seven or eight minutes to go, the floor director said, "Mr. Kinchlow, we'll be on the air soon. Would you take your place, please?"

I thought that *was* my place! Obviously, I was mistaken. Well, maybe they wanted to hear some more of my testimony. So I went over and sat in the guest chair, waiting for Henry and Pat to show up. I was waving at the people in the audience, looking around at the cameras and lights, when the floor director again said, "Excuse me, Mr. Kinchlow, we've got about two minutes before we go on the air. Would you mind taking your place?"

I thought, *Well, this might be a great time to ask where my place is!* So I said, "Well where exactly *is* that?"

The guy looked like somebody punched him in the stomach. "You mean they didn't tell you?"

"Tell me what?"

"Pat and Henry are in Israel! You're the host of the show!"

"What?!!"

Just about that time, the theme music began: *Heaven came down and glory filled my soul!* But at that moment it wasn't glory but *terror* that filled my soul! Henry's recorded "Welcome to the 700 Club" filled the studio and I was on the air, live!

The terror didn't last long. I simply didn't have time to be terrified. I started talking, I interviewed two or three guests, and I managed to keep it up through the next two hours. I don't know how well I did, because mercifully there was no videotape in those days. When Pat returned, he had no evidence of how bad I had been, and the people who invited me sure weren't going to tell, so a few weeks later they called me back to do it again.

The point is, I learned something about myself that day that I never knew before, something I never would have thought possible: By the grace of God, with the power of God, I had hosted a televised talk show on literally a few seconds notice! I had *never* done anything like that before —and it opened my eyes to the possibilities of what could be done in the future. My guest-hosting opportunities eventually led to something I never could have foreseen: a *career* as cohost of "The 700 Club"!

You might say, "Well, that's fine for you, Ben—but what does that have to do with me? There are many things I wish I could do, but I just can't do them. I'm limited by my circumstances, or lack of money, or lack of education, or emotional problems from my childhood, or lack of opportunity or one thing or another. I just can't do it."

That's only true if you allow it to be true! Opportunity is all around you, and exciting, mind-boggling potential is locked up inside you! Yes, you! As a *sovereign, immortal* being, made in the image and likeness of God, you have *unlimited potential* and a destiny beyond description!

Using Your Talents

In New Jerusalem, the Holy City come down from Heaven. Israel will be joined together with the church, the body of Christ, and we shall rule and reign with Christ, face to face with God—*forever*! That is our destiny!

That future destiny should have a profound impact on the way you live your life today. Why? In sin, you come short of the glory of God, and are deflected from the magnificent purpose that God has for your life. You miss the mark of God's glorious destiny in eternity.

But there's more. You see, you don't just fall short of the glory of God when you sin. You also fall short when you are intimidated, when you are paralyzed by fear and doubt. God didn't design you to sit around, bound up by anxiety and worry, your shoes nailed to the floor by such thoughts as, "I can't do this, and I'd sure better not try that." God doesn't limit you. It is you who limits you. And when you limit yourself, you limit what God is able to do in you and through you!

I'm sure you know the story told by Jesus, found in Matthew 25 and Luke 19. In that story, a nobleman is planning a trip to a far country. This nobleman, a biblical type of Jesus, calls his servants together and entrusts them with his goods. To one servant he gave five talents, to another two talents, to another one talent (a talent is a quantity of precious metal, such as silver). He said, "Use these talents until I come back," and he gave each of these servants *sovereign authority* over these talents, each according to his ability.

Now this is a critical point: We don't all receive the same "talents." We don't all have the same abilities, opportunities, background, education, circumstances, and on and on. We are not all the same. God has created us and placed each of us on our own specific level, and He expects us to operate on the cutting edge, the absolute maximum, of that level of talent He has given us. God will never give you more or less than you can fulfill or than will fulfill you.

When the nobleman came back from his trip and demanded an accounting from his servants, the one with five talents said, "I did what you said, I traded those talents on the commodities market, I bought low, sold high, took risks, and now here are your five talents and five more besides." The nobleman said, "Well done, good and faithful servant. You've been faithful in a small thing, now you're ready for bigger things. I shall make you a ruler over ten cities." This servant started out in charge of a few bars of silver, and now he was in charge of ten cities —now that's a promotion!

Then came the second servant. He had been entrusted with less than the first servant, yet like the first servant, he put the entire principal at risk and achieved a 100 percent interest rate, doubling the nobleman's investment. He said, "I maximized what you gave me, I took risks, I invested, and here's your three talents plus three more besides." So the nobleman clapped him on the back and said, "Way to go, bro! You've been faithful in the little things, now it's time for you to step up to the big time. I'm putting you in charge of six cities." Another big promotion! For these two faithful servants, it was like moving straight from the mail room to the governor's mansion!

Then the nobleman came to the last servant, the one

with just one talent. "What did you do with your talent?" he asked. And the servant replied, "Oh, I was scared. You know how risky that commodities market is! I mean, I could have lost it all! I could have failed! I didn't want you getting mad at me, so I played it safe, buried the talent in the ground, and here it is! Aren't you happy?"

Not happy at all! He could have done that himself! He had no interest in a no-interest deal. He expected a return on his investment, but this servant hadn't done one thing to increase his master's net worth. Why? Because he was scared, he was anxious, he was nervous, he was paralyzed by fear. Just like so many people today who are afraid to make a move or take a risk for God, this servant took what his master had given him—and he stuck it in a hole.

What was the nobleman's reaction? "You wicked and lazy servant! Get out of my sight!" The one talent the servant had was then stripped from him and given to the one with ten. Now, what evil thing had this servant done? Had he gone out and committed adultery? No. Stolen anything? No. Murdered anybody? No. He didn't even lose the investment! Yet the nobleman had the unfaithful servant thrown into the outer darkness.

What is God saying to us through this story? "I don't want you sitting around terrified and intimidated, too scared and nervous to make a move." It is the same message He delivers to us in 2 Timothy 1:7—"God has not given us a spirit of craven, cringing fear, but of power, love, and a sound mind." It is the same message Jesus Himself spoke to the disciples when He said, "Let not your heart be troubled, neither let it be afraid" (John 14:27). In other words, don't allow yourselves to be agitated, disturbed, intimidated, fearful, and cowardly!

Freedom from Fear

I used to have a terrible fear of being bitten by a rattle-snake. I'm pretty sure I know where this idea came from: When I was a boy, I was a voracious reader, and I once read a western novel in which there was a scene which stirred up a horrible fear of snakebites that stuck with me well into adulthood. But God never intended for us to be ruled by fear.

One night, while I was attending college by day and driving on the test track at night, the company put me on what we called a "ranch test." The idea was to put the tires to the same kind of use they would undergo on a ranch or farm—a combination of highway driving, dirt roads, and crushed gravel roads. They put me in a pickup, and I would run that truck over a variety of paved and dirt surfaces from 4:00 to 11:00 at night. I'd be driving along, praying in the Spirit, while putting hard miles on those tires.

On one occasion, as I drove and prayed, I saw what appeared to be a huge diamondback rattlesnake lying along the road. Even in the safety of the truck, my flesh began to crawl and I felt a surge of fear. Coming up closer, I saw that the "snake" was really just a big stick. Immense shame washed over me. *God,* I prayed, *will I never be free of this fear?* At that instant, I felt an irresistible urge to stop. Let me tell you, one thing you're not supposed to do out there at night is stop. In fact, there was a specific company policy forbidding it. I wasn't on the regular test track, where another driver would come along shortly. I was all alone out on the ranch track, right in the middle of snake country, and no one else would be out that way till morning. But I just had this overpowering urge to stop, so I stopped. Then I had an urge to open the door, so I opened the door.

I'm not saying God said, "Get out of the truck, Ben," but I felt sure I knew where this compulsion came from. So I gingerly stepped out of the pickup, and—horror of horrors!—I felt an urge to go walking through this pasture in the dark, praying in the Spirit. I thought, *Whoa! This can't be real!* I walked out a little ways, praying and trembling and wondering how many snakes might be surging toward me through the darkness. I had this impression that I was going to run right upon one of those big Texas diamondbacks, but I kept right on walking and praying the more earnestly in the Spirit.

About that time, I felt something come over me, like the blanket of God's presence settling over me. Up to that moment, I had been stepping very carefully, but suddenly I no longer felt a need to be careful. I just began tromping around, praying and praising Jesus! I had a sense that if the snakes were out there, they were all trying like mad to get out of my way! And not only did I *not* step on any snakes, I also didn't stumble over any of the cactus, catclaws, or mesquite bushes that were all around me! (For the record, I don't recommend that anyone else do such a thing!)

Now, I can't prove that there were snakes out there in the darkness, scrambling to get out of my way. All I can prove is that my irrational fear of snakes completely fell away that night—I have no more terror of snakes, just a healthy respect. Years later, I moved out to Chesapeake, in Virginia, and there were a lot of snakes on our property, including some copperheads and water moccasins. A bite from one of those reptiles can ruin your whole day. My wife was terrified of those snakes, but I said, "Hey, don't worry about it. God's going to take care of it." I would walk every day around my back fence for exercise, and sometimes I'd see a water moccasin go slithering along across the tall grass, but I never had any fear. My own lack of fear was small comfort to my wife, so we kept praying that God would do something about those snakes.

Later, I discovered I had two black snakes living up in my barn. I didn't tell my wife (sorry, Dear); she would have made sure those black snakes were properly dispatched. But I decided to leave those black snakes alone and, lo and behold, they cleaned up all the poisonous snakes on my property.

I believe that God often has to bring us to the thing we are afraid of and make us face it. Once we face it, we can move beyond it. But if we never face it, we'll always have to come back to some variation of the thing we fear until we get over it. God is saying to us, "I want to move you beyond your fears. You are one of My own children, and you have no need to fear. I plan to put you in charge of something *big*, and I can't put you in charge of anything if you don't know how to be in charge, if you lack confidence in Me and in your own abilities and decisionability, which I have given you."

This is my favorite story about Smith Wigglesworth, that great apostle of faith of the early twentieth century. Wigglesworth was upstairs in his bedroom, and suddenly he heard a horrendous, unearthly howling. It came from downstairs and rattled the timbers of his house. So he got out of bed, lit his candle, and started downstairs. Halfway down the stairs, he held out his candle and peered into the gloom—and there, in the very middle of his living room, was Satan in all his malevolent majesty!

Smith Wigglesworth looked Satan up and down one time and said, "Oh, it's just you." Then he blew out the candle and went back upstairs to bed.

That's freedom from fear! It is our fear that keeps us in bondage—but God has delivered us from fear through Jesus Christ: "For you did not receive the spirit of bondage again to fear, but you received the Spirit of adoption by whom we cry out, 'Abba, Father'" (Rom. 8:15). When we achieve "the measure of the stature of the fullness of Christ," we do not have to be intimidated by anything! There is power, boldness, and serenity in knowing that God is on our side. We are even free to love those who hate us!

Free to Truly Love

God wants to free us to truly love one another—and to love our enemies. I remember coming across the Lord's "new commandment" in John 13:34—"As I have loved you . . . love one another." That passage gave me a lot of problems in my early Christian life. I thought Jesus was saying, "Ben, I loved you and I was crucified for you. Now I want you to love others as I have loved you. That means you have to be willing to die for others." I have to admit, as much as I loved my kids and my wife and my Christian friends, I wasn't sure I was ready to die in their place. And I *sure* wasn't ready to die for strangers and people who were my enemies!

Here I was, a newly converted black radical, thinking, "God, are You saying I have to be willing to give up my life for some white racist who's been sticking it to my people for all these years? I don't know if I can handle that!" Over the years I had encountered a lot of white people who were clearly the enemies of black people. I'm not just talking about some *nice* white guy like John Corcoran, the man who led me to Christ. I mean bona fide, cross-burning, hood-wearing, red-neck Klansmen! I would read the words of Jesus, "Love your enemies," and I'd think, "You mean them, too? Is *that* who I'm supposed to love?"

Well, is he your enemy?

"Yes!"

Then, Ben, what do you think?

"You gotta be kidding!"

This was part of the internal struggle I was going

through, shortly after I met the Lord Jesus Christ. The Lord was working on me, trying to yank me off this ego trip I had been on as a third-degree black belt martial arts instructor. One day, I was crossing the college campus when I saw this group of hard-looking cowboys. They were standing around in their roughed-out boots and blue jeans, some with cowboy hats, some with caps, one guy with a big ol' beer belly lapping over his belt.

I was walking toward this bunch of riders with my afro sticking out from under my fatigue cap and I could see the situation that was developing as if it were a movie. They were eyeing me, chewing tobacco and spitting, laughing, and carrying on. I knew they were talking about me, and that a confrontation was inevitable.

All right, I thought, *here we go*.

A big fierce grin spread across my face. I was going to give these good ol' boys a lesson in martial arts. Suddenly I stopped—dead in my tracks.

Oh, no, Lord! I thought. *Not them, too!*

Turning my back on those guys was one of the hardest things I ever had to do. They were laughing at me, thinking that this big, bad karate dude had been scared off by a bunch of goat-ropers. I wanted to say, "Excuse me, Lord, I'll be with You in just a minute," then rearrange a few grins, and come back to the Lord very contritely, saying, "God I'm sorry, but You know I couldn't let those guys get away with that!"

But I knew what God was saying to me: "None of that stuff is important anymore—what people think about you, what they call you. It's not your job to defend your own reputation. That's not where you are anymore. You belong to Me. I am your Savior, and I am your Lord. You have surrendered yourself to Me. If you fight, you have divided your allegiance between Me and yourself. A house divided cannot stand. You have to move beyond defending yourself. If you can't do that, you can never be anything, because there will always be small-minded people trying to draw you into a fight. I cannot have that."

Then I understood what God wanted from me—not a willingness to be physically crucified, but a willingness to allow Him to crucify *self*, *pride*, and *ego*, so that I would be free to love others, including my enemies. That's what the surrender of our sovereignty is—a surrender of the rights of self. When God is our defender, when our sovereignty is overshadowed by His sovereignty, then we are free indeed.

Receiving God's Riches

I spoke at a convention in Atlanta, and at the end of the event I was presented with a silver and gold-plated Mont Blanc pen, the kind that costs more than $300. My first response was, "Hey, I can't accept this! I don't deserve this! I use Bics!"

But the man who held out the pen to me said, "Please, take it. We really want you to have it!"

So I accepted it. And I later got to thinking, *This gift isn't about me; it is evidence of their generosity.* This is the way it is between ourselves and God. He wants to give us these wonderful, amazing, exquisite gifts, above and beyond our ability to imagine. Yet we say, "Oh, I can't accept such gifts from God. I don't deserve His gifts." Well, of course we don't deserve them—that's what makes them gifts! They are *charis*, they are grace, they are unearned and undeserved. The gifts of God are not about us; they are additional evidence of God's love and generosity. Therefore, with God-given authority, we come boldly to the throne of His mercy to ask for grace in our time of need. And we can trust Him, knowing that He has promised to supply all our needs according to His riches in glory by Christ Jesus.

I remember well the time I didn't have a job or any money. I had left my job at General Tire Company, and I was "living by faith." My dad, who was also a preacher but employed, questioned my sanity. My wife was beyond questioning—she knew I was crazy!

On this one particular Sunday morning, I was driving my dad to preach at Grace Methodist Church in Del Rio, Texas. All the way over I was real quiet and moody, as I was doing a lot of thinking and praying. I had been getting on my dad ever since I had been baptized in the Holy Spirit and spoke in tongues. I was continually telling him he didn't have it all.

But on the other hand, he had a job and I didn't. That was an eloquent argument in his favor. I was overdrawn at the bank, we had two hungry boys and no food in the house, I only had this raggedy old car and one suit. The bathroom floor had a big hole in it, and I was afraid my children or my wife would fall through. I couldn't afford to fix it, and the landlady wouldn't. We had nothing, we were out of everything, and we had no prospects of things ever getting better. In a word, we were broke.

We got to church, and Dad said, "Well, are you gonna come in?"

I said, "Not right now, Dad. I'm gonna sit out here for a while. I don't feel much like church."

He went into the church to preach and I sat in the car for a while, listening to the hymns wafting from the church. Then I got out and walked around. After a bit, I began to pray, "Lord, I just don't know what to do." I knew it wasn't a matter of something being wrong with God. I just wanted Him to tell me what to do to get myself and my family out of the fix we were in. I had fasted and prayed. I had asked God for insight and guidance. Now I needed help.

I was walking out around the church grounds when, all

of a sudden, I heard a mockingbird. Now, the mockingbird is the state bird of Texas, so there was nothing particularly unusual about hearing a mockingbird. But at that moment, everything else had been so oddly quiet, I couldn't even hear the folks singing in church. What was startling was that everything had been completely still— and then the silence was shattered by this mockingbird.

I kept walking, trying to pray, while that mockingbird sang away, intruding on my thoughts. Finally I thought, "Where is that stupid bird?" I began to look around. I couldn't see him, but I kept hearing him, and it sounded like he was close. Finally, I looked up in the very top of the tallest tree on the church grounds, and up in the top of the tallest tree was this mockingbird.

Have you ever seen a mockingbird? They can mimic the sound of almost every other bird—hence the name. They're kind of roguish birds. They steal eggs, chase other birds, and generally make a nuisance of themselves. This particular bird was on a roll, really into it; he would hit a high note, then fly up in the air like he was really feeling good and praising God. As I watched him, this verse leaped into my mind: "Look at the birds of the air, for they neither sow nor reap nor gather into barns; yet your heavenly Father feeds them. Are you not of more value than they?" (Matt. 6:26).

And I thought, "Yes! That mockingbird has got a Mrs. Mockingbird and some little mockingbirds somewhere, but he ain't worrying about it. He's not worrying about the bank, where his next worm's coming from, or the hole in the floor of his nest. He's just out here, jumping up and down and praising God!"

It was a small thing—yet that incident changed my whole attitude towards God's ability to provide. I realized that if God cares about that mockingbird and his family, then He must care about me and my family.

And that's why God says to all of us: Trust Me! He created us to be sovereign, decisionable, free human beings, and He has set before us a breathtaking horizon of choices. Linked to His mind, His heart, and His power, there is no limit to what we can do and what He can do for us and through us!

Let me ask you: What is the yellow line in your path? Some imaginary limitation or self-doubt? Drive right over it! It can't stop you! It's just a line in your mind! You can if you want to! You don't have to if you don't want to! No one controls you. You are sovereign and immortal. You will live forever. You will never cease to exist. You choose your own destiny. The immense power of choice that God has placed in your hands is terrifying, but it is also exhilarating. You have the responsibility for your own choices and your own actions. This is your life; take hold of it and live it.

"I can if I want to!" Say it to yourself; say it again and again; say it until you believe it; say it until you live it. You will never pass this way again. This is your one and only irreplaceable life. Live it, freely and decisionably, just as God created you to.

The road before you is wide open and limitless. Your adventure with God can begin today. Acknowledge God's provision for eternity with Him, Jesus Christ. Accept His completed work for you and pass from death to life, from separation to union. Of course, you don't have to if you don't want to—but *why* would you not want to?

Your adventure can begin *right now!*—the moment you accept the responsibility and the possibilities of your God-given freedom to choose. This adventure goes on and on throughout eternity. In the ages to come, you can discover vistas and wonders beyond your wildest imaginings —excitement, satisfaction, peace, and superabundant happiness, far above anything you can ask, think, dream, imagine, or aspire to! You can be seated at the right hand of the throne that governs a billion universes, ruling, reigning with unimaginable splendor and power for a thousand million years—

And this is only the beginning. . .

You can if you want to!